Advance Praise

"Danielle Mills's journey was more than just a young girl chasing her professional tennis dream at the Academy. She was a story of grit, endurance, and steadiness. Her commitment opened doors that talent alone never could. Today, she serves as a role model for the IMG Academy girls tennis program, inspiring young female athletes to pursue their goals with the same determination and heart that defined her own path."

—MARGIE ZESINGER, IMG ACADEMY TECHNICAL
DIRECTOR OF WOMEN'S TENNIS

"I've known Danielle since we were kids, and she's never stopped pushing. This memoir captures the same fire and focus she's always had."

—DONALD YOUNG, TWO-TIME GRAND SLAM FINALIST, FORMER
WORLD TOP FORTY, FORMER WORLD NUMBER ONE JUNIOR

"Danielle embodies the mindset, actions, and attitude of a true champion. Even before we met, it was clear she had been forged in the fires of competition and adversity. Success always leaves clues, and Danielle carries them all. Her journey, shaped by experience and exposure at the highest levels, has produced a rare blend of precision, performance, and poise."

—JOHN WILLIAMS, FOUNDER AND CHIEF CLARITY COACH, ELEVATE
WITH JOHN, FORMER COACH OF TAYLOR TOWNSEND WORLD NUMBER
ONE DOUBLES PLAYER, TWO-TIME GRAND SLAM CHAMPION

Scratching the Surface

SCRATCHING THE SURFACE

Lessons from
Bollettieri to
IMG Academy and
the Ways Elite Training
Built a Champion's
Mindset and Shaped
My Journey

DANIELLE MILLS WALDEN

SCRATCHING THE SURFACE

Lessons from Bollettieri to IMG Academy and the Ways Elite
Training Built a Champion's Mindset and Shaped My Journey

FIRST EDITION

ISBN   978-1-5445-5206-4   *Hardcover*
       978-1-5445-5205-7   *Paperback*
       978-1-5445-5207-1   *Ebook*

For the audacity to dream and the courage to pursue those dreams.

For my sweet Otto.

When you're old enough to read this, I hope you see not just your mother's journey but the strength and love that built our family.

You are the legacy I'm most proud of.

CONTENTS

AUTHOR'S NOTE

This book is a true account of my life and experiences, told through my own perspective. I have done my best to recall events, conversations, and emotions as accurately as possible. The story reflects how I experienced and interpreted those moments at the time they occurred.

While most names, events, and locations are accurate depictions of real people and experiences, some have been changed or altered to protect privacy and maintain confidentiality. Any resemblance to individuals not intentionally included is purely coincidental.

Memory is inherently personal, and while I have made every effort to ensure honesty and authenticity, this work should be read as my recollection and reflection—not as a verified record of every detail.

The thoughts and opinions expressed are solely my own and do not represent the views of any organizations, employers, or affiliations, past or present.

BEFORE I WAS A PRO

$$1$$

THE SELECTION

Bradenton, Florida, was nothing like upstate New York. It was hot. Sticky. Here on the Gulf Coast, it would never be cold. And for the first time in my life, I'd be playing tennis outside year-round.

Eighty people—mostly teens—gathered on Court five at IMG Academy, a private preparatory boarding school and sports training academy. Orientation at IMG kicked off with a selection process. We'd be divided into groups and assigned coaches. Seven years of practice and tournaments had led up to this moment, and I was ready. After all, I'd done well in New York, earned a state ranking, and was number one in my region for the under-twelve-year-olds when I was eleven years old. This meant that you could play in this age class until you turned thirteen years old. But I was always "playing up" since I was nine to eleven years old playing in the twelve-and-under division. I was on my way to the big leagues. My parents believed it, and I believed it too.

The night before orientation, I received a pamphlet about selection. The instructions were basic: when and where to meet, along with a cursory description of the process. Once placed in a group, I would practice with those kids and that coach for the entire school year. Reading that pamphlet, I thought, *This will determine my fate.* I was happy and excited but also fearful. *What if I end up in the wrong group?* I brushed the thought aside. After all, I was a winner. I'd been proving myself competitively since I was five years old, and nothing stood in the way between me and success.

At eleven years old (*going on twelve,* I liked to remind myself), I was the youngest person on the court, but at a lanky five seven and ninety-seven pounds, I was still taller and skinnier than many of the other girls. I wondered if my height made me look older, more mature. Like a professional. My pink glasses, sliding down my nose with sweat in the Florida heat and humidity, sure didn't.

I was also one of the few Black girls on the court. Still, there was more cultural diversity here than I'd ever experienced back in Rochester. As we stood there waiting for selection to begin, I could hear kids speaking different languages. Even though I didn't know any of the other kids, I was already feeling at home. We were all different, but we were all tennis players. For the first time in my life, I felt like I belonged.

I looked around at the other students. Boys and girls from eleven to eighteen all stood on the court waiting to be selected. We eyed each other up and down, sizing up the "competition."

In my mind, I was already dividing them into groups. The legitimate players had the right clothing, several high-quality rackets, a racket bag, and all the other equipment a serious tennis player carried. Other kids looked like amateurs, hanging onto just one racket, no bag, and sort of disorganized, like they didn't know what they were doing or even why they were there. I stood tall and confident in full sports attire: a tennis shirt, skirt, sneakers, and visor. Four rackets and a bag. I was on time and prepared—habits my dad had instilled in me at a young age. I hoped they would serve me well on this very important day.

Like me, the level of professionalism and skill with which the other students viewed themselves showed in their posture, how they walked, talked, and looked at each other and the coaches. Little did we know that all that would change after the selection process, where we'd be divided not by gear, but by skill level. And skill level was based on one metric: results. Where we placed in ranked region, state, national, and world tournaments would determine our immediate future at IMG.

While our clothing and gear varied, we all had one thing in common: a gallon jug of ice water with the name "Bollettieri" on it—a reference to the original owner of this sports playground. This was mandatory equipment for surviving the Southern heat. I had picked up my jug at the pro shop that morning, located one of the many huge ice machines around the campus, and filled it up. My mom had been with me, but she wasn't here now. Neither was my dad. It was a rare moment when they weren't watching over me, and it felt odd, but it also felt good. Like freedom.

I spent much of the summer at the Academy. My parents had sent me there for a week, then two weeks, and then three weeks before deciding to enroll me for the full-time school year. So I was familiar with some of the coaches, and I knew which group I wanted to be in: Percy Melzi's. His current group wasn't around during the summer because they were traveling and playing in tournaments around the world. Being selected for Coach Percy's new group of students, and more importantly, being coached by him as my group head coach, could have an enormous impact on my future in tennis. Those girls were prodigies.

I scanned the crowd and spotted a few familiar faces among the coaches. There was Percy, the top girls coach, and Mark Dalzell, the top boys coach. The assistant coaches hung around the fringes while the dozen or so head coaches stood front and center. Just one coach, Paul Forsyth, nodded at me in recognition and said hi, but the rest looked serious and avoided eye contact. The head coaches zeroed in on certain students, as if they already sort of knew who would be in their groups. None of them were staring at me. And for the first time that morning, standing outside on Court five in the brilliant Florida sunshine, with all the right training and gear, my eleven-year-old self wondered if I'd done enough. If I was good enough to join the elite ranks of young girls vying for a chance to train with the top coach at the top sports school. Ultimately, if *I* was enough—worthy of being among the chosen few to earn a spot in the professional world of women's tennis.

GETTING INTO IMG

My parents had learned about IMG Academy in the 1980s, when the school was called Bollettieri Tennis Academy. If you wanted your kid to play professionally, or at least at the Division I level, you sent them to Bollettieri.

Mom and Dad loved tennis. When my mother became pregnant with me, she and my dad decided if they had a daughter, that girl would play tennis. So even before I was born, I was destined to be a tennis player. There's a rumor that the name Gabriela was on the table—for me to be named after Gabriela Sabatini, a player my parents liked. But they ultimately went with Danielle. To think I could have been named after a professional player! It's like fate.

Growing up in upstate New York, I had some competition success in the Western New York region, which was made up of Rochester, Buffalo, Syracuse, and Binghamton. I was ranked number one in that region out of all the girls. That made up my parents' minds: I was going to the Academy! They wanted to give me the best shot at achieving my dreams. Or rather, *their* dream because I wasn't interested in tennis. As a child and a preteen, I always wanted to play soccer. All the cool kids at school played soccer. But my parents pushed me into tennis, and I went along with it. And did well, despite feeling isolated and alone. Nobody else at my school played tennis, and I experienced mild bullying because of being different.

My dad knew all about IMG, but I'd never heard of it. One day while I was playing in the basement, he and my mom came downstairs and sat me down for what seemed like a pretty serious conversation. They told me about this sports boarding school in Florida. They were excited about sending me there but also apprehensive about whether I could handle it on my own.

"This is a big opportunity for you, Danielle. Don't get in any trouble," my dad said. My mom echoed that sentiment, and it confused me. Get in trouble? I was the last kid to get in any trouble!

"I don't know what you mean, but okay," I said.

"Listen to the people in charge. Pay attention. Follow the rules." My dad looked at me sternly, and Mom nodded in agreement. Okay, they weren't kidding.

That still seemed funny to me because I was, and still am, the biggest rule-follower I know. I always want to understand how to play the game. And I'm not rebellious. I thrive in structured environments because the rules are clear. To succeed, all I have to do is follow them.

At eleven years old, I'd never gone anywhere besides school without my parents. They talked to people at the Academy and were convinced it was a safe environment. Still, sending me away for an entire school year was risky. As a test, they sent me there to train for a week during the Academy's summer camp. I flew down to Florida with my tennis coach at the time, Emelie Fauchet, and her kids, Sebastien and Jean-Philippe (J.P.), who were also enrolled in the camp. They were top ranked in my region, and back then, I looked up to their level and skill. My parents saw that, and even back then, they were connecting me with coaches who could take me to a higher level than where I was. When I came back and told them how much I loved the place, they sent me back for another two weeks, and then three more. All that summer, I was sold on IMG Academy, and so were my parents.

I had just finished fifth grade in upstate New York, where middle school starts with sixth grade. Since I hadn't settled into a new school with a new group of friends yet, the timing was perfect for me to become a full-time IMG student.

The Academy was intrigued by the idea of allowing a kid my age into their tennis program, but also cautious. They wanted to make sure an eleven-year-old could handle boarding school life on her own. Many eleven-year-old kids still need a ton of guidance from their parents, and rightfully so, but I didn't act like that. Carolina Murphy, one of the head directors of the full-time program, interviewed me on the phone. I took the call from the basement in our home while my parents waited in another room. I remember being nervous and excited for this conversation. She asked me a lot of questions to gauge my interest, excitement, and maturity. I must have impressed her because the school soon notified my parents that they would make an exception for me. I was in!

To say I was excited is an understatement. I wasn't just excited to be going to IMG. I was euphoric. I was going to Florida for a whole school year! My recent memories of those glorious weeks at summer camp were fresh, and I could taste the freedom in the air. The idea of living on campus full time was almost too good to imagine. I'd gotten a big taste of freedom, of being around other young tennis players—rooming with them, eating with them, playing against them—during those early summer weeks. The thought of living the dorm life like a college student, and almost like an adult, was incredible. Plus, I'd get to play tennis outside every day, even through the winter. This was something I'd never experienced in Rochester, where you must play indoors eight months a year, which really limited my game and my exposure to different surfaces like clay and grass.

Living in upstate New York, I was used to gray skies, rain, and snow. We were lucky to get two months of decent weather the whole year. In Florida, every day was sunny. I could play tennis outside in the fresh air year-round.

Indoor and outdoor tennis are very different. Inside, the environment is controlled. There's heat and air conditioning—perfect conditions. Outside, you're dealing with the elements. The sun, clouds, wind, and temperature affect how you play. Indoors, it's all about skill. Out in the heat, a player who can outlast their opponent has a tremendous advantage. Physical fitness and endurance can mean the difference between a win and a loss. Florida was my chance to work on the physical aspects of the sport and improve my game.

I'd miss my parents, but I was sure they'd visit me when they could. In the meantime, I'd be Miss Independent, making her way in the world of tennis. What I didn't know was that my parents had already planned to move to Florida to be near me.

SELECTION BEGINS

For the second time in twenty-four hours, I brushed any doubts and negative thoughts aside and focused on all I had done to get into the Academy. All the training, the sacrifices. Forcing a smile, I stood straighter, taller. I was ready for this. Ready to join the ranks of the top girls at IMG.

Paul Forsyth moved to the front of the coaches, signaling the start of the selection process. Conversations faded to murmurs, then silence.

Paul's voice boomed above the crowd. "Is there anyone here who is unranked?"

A few girls and boys raised their hands. Another coach came forward and waved them over. "Okay, I need you all to come with me. You're in the great Cougar's group."

Unranked? I felt sorry for those kids. They were in the lowest-performing group by level, with a coach apparently used to working with unranked players. Not that any of IMG's coaches were bad, and that particular coach was super friendly and very nice to me, but compared to Percy and some of the others, he was not the coach *I* wanted to be with because of *the players* he was coaching. I watched as he led his team of "unrankeds" off the court. They had no reason to stick around. In retrospect, coaching lower-level players is extremely challenging and should be admired much more. Many players arrive at IMG already at a high level, and it's just about refinement. When you have to take a player who's not very skilled and turn them into a D1 athlete in one or two years, that should be applauded more.

Paul spoke again. "Who has a state or national ranking?" Now they were talking! I proudly stepped forward. Along with a lot of other students. I wondered how they would separate us. The answer was soon clear.

"Okay, and who has an ITF world ranking?" I didn't have an ITF world ranking at the time. But other girls and boys did, and they quickly separated themselves from our group. A tightness rose in my chest. This was not what I expected.

It only got worse from there.

The head coaches moved in to divide each group further and claim their students. I was pulled into Jairo Aldana's group. I didn't know what that meant, but the coach appeared to be super nice and friendly. I noticed there were girls and boys in his group so that took me by surprise.

That morning, coming to orientation and selection, I knew Coach Percy trained only the best of the best girls from around the world. And I thought I belonged among them. But now I saw that not only did *I* not qualify, *but no one on the court that day was good enough for his elite group of tennis players.*

Later, I learned that Percy's group of girls all had world rankings and were among the top ten in their age group in their respective countries and around the world. Some were in the top five. Some were even playing up in their age group—playing against grown women in the ITF eighteen-and-under tournaments. From my understanding, none of them paid to be there. They were on schol-arships or were signed by IMG, the tennis experience for them and their families covered by the Academy. It was a small group of elite players—fewer than a dozen—and three-quarters of them were already represented by agents. People believed these girls could become the next best players in the world. Coach Percy's students weren't on Court five that day because they had already been hand-picked to train with the top girls coach at IMG. Percy, as well as the top boys coach, Mark, had shown up to see if they had missed any ITF-ranked players from among this new batch of students who might be worthy to join their group. A few boys qualified to join the boys' top group, but no girls left with Coach Percy.

I also learned there was a group *above* Percy's. Nick Bollettieri, the founder of IMG Academy, had his own group of girl students who were also pros. In my mind, that group was so far beyond the realm of possibility I couldn't even imagine being invited to join. I would never be good enough to train with Nick. I set my sights on Coach Percy's group. It was a dream, but for now, it was all I had.

Looking around at the other groups, I noticed they were separated, all boys or all girls under the best coaches. Then I looked at my group. A mix of ten boys and girls lumped together. I looked at my head coach, Jairo. He was a great coach, but he wasn't coaching the top girls. I thought I had done everything to succeed at IMG, yet there I was. I had learned I was in the second-to-lowest group by skill on the court. My state ranking had saved me from the embarrassment of being in the lowest-skilled group—but just barely. My smile was gone.

The only saving grace was that I was the youngest in the group. We even had a seventeen-year-old playing at my eleven-year-old level. I was grasping at straws at that point, looking for any signs of hope. And I realized I was not where I wanted to be, where I expected to be. Where I thought I deserved to be. But I had a rude awakening because I learned that your proximity to greatness is only based on who is in your environment. Back in New York, I was number one, the best. But compared to who? This is something I tell parents who ask me about their kids competing. I always say it's so important to expose your children to the best in the world so they never have their egos bruised the way mine was. In retrospect, the experience pushed me to fight, but at the time, I was broken and hurt by not living up to what I thought my level was. It was a wake-up call for sure.

I was cordial to my group and smiled and said hello to the other boys and girls. But it was tough to hide my disappointment. This might be a pleasant group of tennis players, but I did not want to be a part of it. This was the first time in my life I felt like I didn't belong— and that I needed to do something to change my reality.

I was so far down from where I needed to be to get where I wanted to go. My next thought was, *What was I going to do about it?*

2

THE ARRIVAL

Even before I was accepted to IMG full time, my father was probably talking to a Florida realtor. He and my mom bought a house about five blocks from the Academy. I was confused at first—and not exactly thrilled. Why would they move to Florida? I wanted to be on my own. They explained that I would live on campus Monday through Friday and at home with them every weekend.

I understood why they wanted to be close to me. I was eleven years old! No matter how mature I felt, I was still a kid. A tall, skinny, awkward kid who couldn't wait to play tennis year-round in sunny Florida. Still, with Mom and Dad just a stone's throw away, I felt as if my independence was threatened.

They drove me to school that first day, just like they would every Sunday evening for the next seven years. I showed up at the Academy with everything on the school's list of supplies. Along with my usual school clothes, tennis outfits, and gear, I had all the Bed, Bath, and Beyond necessities: sheets, towels, and other home essentials. It was like moving into my first college dormitory because that's exactly what it was: a dorm but with the feel of a small apartment. Zipping off the plastic on my first twin-size bed comforter, I noted the smell and reminded myself to wash all the bedding before putting it on my bunk. This was my first bunk bed and my first bedroom with roommates. I chose the top bunk, I think because I liked the idea of using the lower bunk for storage. If this was going to be a new experience, I wanted to try it all. My roommate, Taylor Schreimann, was from Dallas, Texas. She was in the bunk across from mine. I guess they could have fit four girls into one room like they had during the summer program, but during the full-time year it was just Taylor and me. We immediately bonded over tennis and how excited we were to be eleven and twelve years old at this very big campus. While we were similar, we were worlds different. She liked country music and was a huge Taylor Swift fan. Yes, even back then, Taylor Swift was making an impact. She would sing songs like "Tim McGraw" and "Teardrops on My Guitar" while I was focused on rap music and trying desperately to learn all the lyrics to Missy Elliot's *Under Construction* and Ludacris's *Word of Mouf* albums.

My mom taught me how to use the alarm clock. Up until then, I had relied on my parents to wake me up every morning for the most part. My mom would come into my bedroom in Rochester and say, "Danielle, it's time to get up." I didn't like waking up early, but it was something I needed to do to catch the seven o'clock school bus back in Rochester, so here at IMG, I knew it would be similar. In the bathroom, I hung a shower caddy and arranged all my personal stuff, including a new toothbrush and toothpaste, shampoo, and brushes. I'd be sharing the bathroom with other girls, so I was careful to keep my things together and leave room for their supplies. Being an only child, sharing my space was all new to me, but I had been raised to be considerate of other people. I wasn't a stereotypical, self-centered, spoiled kid—or at least that was what people told me. They would say, "Wow, you don't have only-child energy." Whatever that meant. I always assumed it meant I wasn't selfish. Instead, I was excited to be around other kids, not just in the classroom and on the court but all day.

Once my room was set up, it was time for my parents to leave.

"Well, this is it, Danielle." My dad looked me in the eye and gave me a final hug.

"You're going to do great, honey," said my mom. I could always count on her support, and though I didn't need it at that moment, it still felt good to hear. I watched them leave and stood alone in that room. Just me, no one else. No teachers, no parents, and for now, no other students. From now on, I was responsible for myself. Maybe I should have been scared, but I wasn't. It was the beginning of everything I wanted. The start of my life as a serious tennis player. And the first real moment of true freedom because let's be honest: this environment was not what an eleven-year-old was accustomed to. But it would change my life.

STUDENT ORIENTATION

IMG orientation for new full-time students is an every-year thing, no matter how many years you attend the school. Unlike tennis orientation, kids from all the sports were there, along with their parents. Keep in mind at this time IMG had baseball, basketball, soccer, golf, hockey, and tennis. In a room full of teenagers, moms, and dads, at eleven years old, I was the youngest. I sized up the room, the parents, and the students. Most of the students were in high school, but a few had graduated and were spending a gap year at IMG before heading to college. They called them "postgrads," and I immediately noticed how old they appeared. At eighteen or nineteen, they were much older than I was.

We gathered in the auditorium where Gary Cohen, the head of the full-time program at the time, addressed us. He wore one of those funny Britney Spears-type microphones and a small fanny pack with a speaker.

"Welcome to IMG," he boomed. "You are in for the greatest experience and opportunity of your lives. Your parents have sent you here, and I know you all appreciate them and will make the most of your time here."

It was like a pep rally speech laced with a subtle warning that we'd better not screw up.

"I'm looking around this room," he continued, "and I know for a fact that not everybody sitting here today will be here at the end of the year."

That got my attention.

"A number of you will leave the Academy because of decisions you make and rules you break."

Okay, I thought, *they take the rules very seriously*. My father gave me one of those stern looks, like, "You'd better not mess this up." My mom glanced around. I gulped spit.

Gary explained the many IMG rules, and I did my best to memorize them, though I figured they were written somewhere in the orientation packet. There were a lot of them. Students were only allowed to be with a member of the opposite sex in communal areas, such as outside, by the pool, and in the cafeteria. Never in the dormitories. They were serious enough about this rule to have a camera stationed at the entryway of every dorm building floor. There was a curfew, too: anyone under the age of sixteen had to be in their dorm room by eight o'clock, with lights out by nine, while other students could stay out until nine but had to be in bed by ten o'clock. They did dorm checks, too—with a flashlight full-on in your face at two o'clock or four o'clock in the morning—to make sure you were in your bed before the curfew, but more to ensure you were alone, with no other boys or girls in your bed.

IMG was a smoke-free campus. No smoking, no alcohol, and definitely no drugs. There would be random drug tests. Without warning, you would have to go to the mental conditioning building to be met by the drug test administrators and stay there until you could pee. So if you made the mistake of peeing beforehand, get ready to drink a bunch of water and stay there for hours until you could pee, but more on that later. Sure enough, the rules were in the handbook, and each student had to sign their copy.

One rule in particular came up again and again at IMG: the "in the presence of" rule. Gary made that rule very clear and repeated it twice to ensure everyone in the room, including the parents, understood the repercussions of it. This was a no-refunds academy, so if you broke a rule and got expelled, they would not be giving Daddy a refund.

"Throughout your time here," Gary said, "you will see other students break the rules. If you are *in the presence of* someone doing anything illegal or breaking an IMG rule, you must call this number, which I want you to put in your phones right now. No matter where you are, an IMG staff member will come pick you up and bring you to your dorm, no questions asked."

Gary continued.

"But if you are around people doing these things, even if you are not involved, and you don't remove yourself or call us to come and get you, and we catch you or find out you were there after the fact, you'll be treated the same as the people engaged in those activities. That could mean getting an infraction against you or even being expelled with no refund."

What horrible things could a kid do to get them expelled? My mind couldn't even go there. I memorized the number and hoped I'd never have to call it. Up until then, I'd only called my parents on my little Nokia phone. I wasn't allowed to call anyone else or send text messages at all. Back then, unlimited texting didn't exist. We had to pay for every text message. One month, I went over my allotted fifty messages and got into a lot of trouble with my dad, who paid my phone bill—and made it clear that texting was a privilege.

Gary was still talking. "I would hate to see any of you sitting in my office with Carolina Murphy, the 'Discipline Committee,' and having to call your parents to let them know that you've been expelled from *the Academy*."

He was trying to get us to imagine what that would feel like, and it was working. Parents looked at their kids like, "You'd better never call me with that news." I didn't make eye contact with my parents. As an extreme goodie-two-shoes rule-follower, I was terrified. This rule changed my life.

While everyone else had a concerned look on their face, I was smiling, happy, and excited to be there. Nothing Gary said applied to me. No drugs, no smoking, no alcohol, no problem. I didn't do any of those things. I loved rules. They showed me how to play the game and how to win it. I loved structure. It was what I knew. My parents had had rules for everything my whole life. This was no different. Other kids looked terrified. Especially the high school and postgrad kids.

Gary explained the daily schedule. Everyone had to be up and out of their dorm by six in the morning. We'd eat breakfast in the cafeteria, fill our jugs with ice water, and then, depending on our particular sport and schedule, rotate through training, playing, and academics in the classroom. Our only break was lunch at noon in the cafeteria and at the end of the day when dinner was over.

MY DAILY SCHEDULE

I learned my schedule quickly. Up by five thirty; shower, dress, and head to the cafeteria for breakfast. I had physical conditioning at six thirty, followed by tennis, private lessons, more tennis, and more private lessons until eleven. Then more physical conditioning, followed by lunch and, finally, two hours of classroom time. After school, there were two more hours of tennis and then mental conditioning or other tennis-related training. Dinner was at five, and then I had a few hours to socialize before curfew. With the tight schedule, I had to plan ahead. I laid out the next day's clothes before going to bed at night to save precious minutes in the morning.

Going between my dorm and the cafeteria, gym, classrooms, and tennis courts took time; this was a massive campus that was acres large. Once I figured out the campus, I realized there was no way I could make it to all these places on time. That explained why all the younger students tooled around on Razor scooters. My parents got me one too. In the years to come, I gave up my scooter for a bike. Eventually, I started riding a golf cart like the ones that transported the other kids all around the campus.

Think of a college campus with different buildings and training facilities. On foot it could take you thirty minutes to get from one side to another. On a scooter, maybe ten. On a bike, five, and on a golf cart—because of all the stops—probably ten minutes. But these were all things I would have to factor into planning my day. Nobody was holding my hand and making sure I was okay. I had to learn this. I was forced to be mature and act like an adult who had a busy schedule without my parents' direction. Remember, they were in their house Monday through Friday, and I was on this campus, navigating this world alone.

THE STRUCTURE AT IMG VERSUS LIVING AT HOME

As structured as the schedule was, IMG was more liberal than what I was used to. At home, I never left my house except to get on the school bus or go somewhere with my parents. Here, I could walk between buildings, go to the pool by myself, or just hang out on campus with my friends. As long as I stayed within the boundaries of the Academy, stuck to the schedule, and followed the rules, I was free to wander and do as I pleased. The analogy I'd like to give you is that it was like a sandbox I was free to play in that was safe and controlled. As I was in the sandbox, I was okay.

I wondered how my parents would manage their work schedules so far from New York. Sure enough, they had planned that too. Mom sold her insurance business, and Dad kept the house in Rochester and continued working both in the office and remotely. Mom worked for him, too, before she owned her own insurance agency. Before COVID-nineteen, working remotely wasn't common. When other students asked how my parents could be at IMG every day and still hold down their businesses, I tried to explain, but I don't think they understood. To be honest, I still don't know how they pulled it off, but they did. When they wanted something bad enough, they figured out a way to make it happen. That was my parents. They always made sure they did what they needed to do from a business standpoint to be able to show up fully for me all those years. They constantly flew back and forth between Rochester, New York, and Bradenton, Florida.

Their careful planning allowed them to visit the school almost every day. Sometimes they showed up for practice sessions with my group, and sometimes they came just for my private lessons. They liked to watch the practice sets and the games too. They might stay for just the first couple of hours, go home, and then come back later for my afternoon sessions.

They weren't the only parents to show up for their kids, even though at times it felt like that. The most talented tennis players in Coach Percy's group had been signed by agents, and their parents had quit their jobs or left their careers to be with their children as they moved through the process of turning pro. It was comparable to a child actor or musician, where the parent drops everything to be there in support of but is indebted to the agent and/or label representing the kid. But in my group, Coach Jairo's group, the second-to-lowest skill level group at that time, only my parents sat in the bleachers, drinking Gatorade and watching my every move. Sometimes their presence irritated me. Other times I appreciated the support. Regardless, how I felt about them being there didn't matter. They weren't going anywhere. Even when I expressed annoyance or discomfort, I didn't have the heart to share how I really felt. I was a kid, and I figured they would pick up on my facial expressions and my body language. They didn't. I think them being there can be attributed to them not having much support in person from their own families growing up and playing sports. So they wanted to do everything they felt they didn't get. As a parent now, I totally understand. Looking back, I hate that this bothered me so much; it was less about them being there and being supportive and more about how other kids and coaches made me feel because they knew being there meant they had money or enough success to be there. That changed how the kids viewed me.

Oddly enough, my parents had never shown up for my practices in Rochester. My mother would pick me up from school, drop me off at the Midtown Athletic Club, and pick me up later. She would sometimes work out in the gym while I was practicing with my first "official" private coach, Ron Dyson. He laid the foundation for a few pivotal years from when I was about five to eight years old. Then I switched to working with Emelie Fauchet until I moved to IMG at eleven years old. Once we were in Florida, my parents took my tennis career much more seriously, and I can't blame them. IMG is a *huge* financial investment, but they would do anything it took to get me to reach my fullest potential.

IMG ACADEMY: THE ORIGINAL SPORTS BOARDING SCHOOL

In 1978, Nick Bollettieri founded what was then known as Nick Bollettieri Tennis Academy, the first sports boarding school ever established.[1] What began as a school for tennis hopefuls came to serve as a blueprint for all other sports boarding schools that opened after its inception.

In 1987, IMG purchased the Academy, renamed the school, and added golf, soccer, baseball, hockey, and basketball to the lineup. In 2010, football was added and in 2013, lacrosse and track and field. Today volleyball, swimming, and soon wrestling are part of the Academy's offerings. There are no limits. I wouldn't be surprised if more sports continue to be added. IMG is a sports and entertainment agency company that represents actors, models, and athletes. When an IMG athlete signs a professional contract, the agent gets a cut, and IMG gets a cut. When an athlete gets a pro deal, such as a contract with a sports clothing company like Nike or Adidas, the agent and IMG get a cut. This is how the school supports scholarship students. In 2023, a company called Endeavor bought the Academy for $1.2 billion, but the IMG name stayed because of the name recognition. Some tennis enthusiasts, who are more so baby boomers, still refer to IMG as "Bollettieri's." Nick Bollettieri is arguably the most famous, most successful tennis coach in the world.

The Academy is known as "the world's toughest playground," and top players from around the world trained—and still train—there, expecting to receive a Division I college scholarship as the bare minimum and become professional athletes. Division I is the highest level of collegiate sports, comprising major universities and regulated by the NCAA (National Collegiate Athletic Association). There are lower levels, such as Division II and Division III. Less than two percent of high school graduates play at the highest level, and only two percent of Division I women's tennis players go pro.

IMG was set up to produce Division I and professional players, with state-of-the-art facilities and some of the top coaches in the world. That came with a hefty price tag for non-scholarship students, close to six figures annually, not including the academic portion of the boarding school. For this reason, most students attended the Academy for a year or two. Few stayed year after year, and I don't know of anyone who attended as long as I did, from sixth grade through high school.

A WHO'S WHO OF STUDENTS

Nick Bollettieri is credited with developing twenty-five number-one-ranked ATP and WTA (men and women circuit) players. The man, Nick, and now the Academy create champions. Grand Slam winners. Name a successful tennis player who played from the 1970s to the present, and you can trace their training to the original sports academy, IMG, and often to Nick Bollettieri.

The list of tennis pros who attended IMG is long: Andre Agassi, Monica Seles, Jim Courier, Kei Nishikori, Donald Young, Mary Pierce, Tommy Haas, Max Mirnyi, Sandra Cacic, Madison Brengle, Heather Watson, Sabine Lisicki, Anna Kournikova, Serena and Venus Williams, Maria Sharapova, and many, many more. In addition to tennis players, other prominent athletes who attended the Academy while I was training there included Major League Soccer players Freddy Adu, Jozy Altidore, Brek Shea, Landon Donovan, Eddie Johnson, and

Josh Lambo; men's professional basketball players Michael Beasley, Dwight Powell, Ricky Sánchez, Ramel Bradley, and Taurean Green; women's DI basketball player Moniquee Alexander; golfers Jessica and Nelly Korda (who were are also my neighbors growing up near IMG); and baseball players John Ryan (JR) Murphy, Paolo Espino, Blaze Alexander, and L.J. Mazzilli, along with many more. These players were ones who I was in school with at IMG and I saw on a regular basis. Not listed are all the pro athletes who used IMG as their offseason home base or basketball or football players who used it for their combine or pro day preparations. Basically it was where you went to prepare for your draft. A quick Google search of professional athletes who train or trained at IMG brings you to a Wikipedia page that is truly a who's who of athletes.

LIFE ON CAMPUS

The Academy became a mecca for men's and women's sports training. Everyone was glad to be there. The players had dreams of becoming Division I athletes and playing professionally. For kids like me, IMG was the playground that could make our dreams come true.

IMG was about 190 acres when I attended and included a pool, a cafeteria, offices, classrooms, a gym for physical strength and mental conditioning training, more than forty tennis courts, and fields for all the other sports. There were indoor tennis courts in the Bollettieri Dome, one of just two places to play indoors in Florida at the time. If it rained, we played in the Dome. Today, the campus takes up over 600 acres.

As fancy as the training areas were, the living quarters at IMG left much to be desired. The dormitory buildings were lettered A through K. Each building had two floors and no elevator. The dormitories were old and worn down, and each building contained eight miniature apartments, or dorms. Each dorm had a small room with a sink, table, couch, and TV. Past this shared area were two bedrooms with two bunk beds each, and beyond those, two bathrooms.

Depending on the time of year, up to four girls or boys shared each dorm room. Students were separated by gender but not by sport. I shared rooms with one to three golfers, basketball players, and soccer players of different ages. Dorm rules were strict. No boys in the girls' dorms, and vice versa. Cameras at the entrances kept track of who came in and out. Food was allowed, which I could bring back from the cafeteria, purchase from the cafe, or get from a supermarket during a weekend trip into town or to my parents' house.

During my first two years on campus, a dorm mother, Karen McDonald, kept an office inside my dorm, B-101. This was to ensure I had eyes on me and if I needed anything there was an adult present. Karen was a heavier-set woman who had a distinct slow walk. She moved around the dorms slowly, but you knew she was coming. A St. Louis native, she had a strong accent. She rode a motorcycle, and she always talked about her riding friends. I think she was in a biking club. She ended up passing away in 2012 after some health issues. Later, as I got a little older, dorm staff like Marlene and Kelly kept an eye on us girls. These women got to know the students well and were always looking out for their well-being. Marlene was Puerto Rican, and we bonded over our culture and the fact that she had so many beautiful daughters. One of her daughters, Damaris, attended the Pendleton School at IMG with me but was a grade older. She used to take me on these really fun golf cart rides through the campus and up and around the golf course. I can still feel the breeze through my hair as we zoomed around.

Kelly was my other favorite dorm staff. She had a daughter who was a bit younger than me, but I always thought that maybe I reminded her of her daughter since I was also "mixed." Kelly was tall and played high school volleyball. She was really good at giving advice and just being an overall amazing person. She really tried to teach and protect a lot of the girls since we were on a campus of mostly teenage boys, so you know how that can be when you are dealing with a bunch of kids with raging hormones and emotions. Coming from my parents' home, the dorms were a step down in my living conditions; they weren't in a new building by any means, but I wasn't there to hang out. I was at IMG to play tennis.

The Academy did its best to room girls in the same age range together, but with me being just eleven, that wasn't possible. So I got to hang out with some older teenagers. You might think a kid my age would struggle to fit in, but I was always naturally outgoing and very mature for my age. My parents had exposed me to a lot of travel and experiences, so being in a new situation didn't faze me at all. I made friends quickly. I felt like my entire life—all eleven years of it—had led me to this point, and I was ready to embrace it.

During summer camp and that first year at IMG, I met students from around the world. My roommates were from Spain, New Zealand, Kuwait, Poland, Australia, Portugal, Venezuela, Brazil, Russia, and many other countries. Some of them didn't speak English, but others were bilingual, which was new to me! Other than my mother, who's Puerto Rican, I had never been around people like this, and the multicultural environment made me feel more connected to my culture as a Latina. This is where my passion for languages and culture really began. I loved learning new languages, and I prided myself in trying to learn a couple of phrases in every language. It was a way for me to bond with them and perfect my accent.

The energy on campus was electric. Walking around, you could taste the unmasked potential in the air. Every student had a look in their eye like they were on a mission. There was a sense of urgency and purpose. People were always doing something and going somewhere. You didn't see students just standing around. Smartphones weren't a thing yet, so everyone wore a watch. Being on time mattered. Being present mattered. To be honest, being on time meant you were late but more on that later.

Nearly every student was excited to be there. Some were super talented and attended on scholarships, and others, like me, played well but not well enough to merit a scholarship. Our parents paid for our tuition, training, room, and board, most likely offsetting the costs for scholarship kids to attend. Even back then, IMG wasn't a cheap boarding school. Attending the Academy full-time cost somewhere between $75,000 and $100,000 a year. Schooling cost another $15,000 to $20,000.

There were a few outliers—primarily kids from wealthy families who came from countries where their safety was at risk. Their parents put them into IMG to protect them, and the students obviously did not want to be there. IMG offered those families a secure environment for their children. The campus was gated and protected from outsiders. Security guards and staff members walked around with walkie-talkies. No one who wasn't supposed to be there got in. You would stick out like a sore thumb if you didn't belong.

Before IMG, my whole life was spent with my parents, but it's not like they kept me locked away in a tower. Mom and Dad took me everywhere with them. I got used to being around their adult friends. Traveling the world with them on their insurance award trips, I was often the only child in a room full of adults. That meant entertaining myself with coloring books or toys. It meant being polite and not interrupting their conversations. As an only child, I was afforded a lot of opportunities that others weren't, but being in those spaces demanded a level of maturity. Looking back, I'm glad I was there, but it did contribute to why I didn't relate as well to kids my age.

At the Academy, I was surrounded by hundreds of teens and pre-teens from around the world. We were all young, and we all played sports. Boys and girls. Golfers, soccer players, baseball players, basketball players, and tennis players. Hauling gear from one building to the next. And training. Always training. Always competing.

An only child, I had never spent time alone with other young people except in elementary school. There was always a teacher or a coach around. The Academy gave me a true social life. This was my first opportunity to form deep friendships. We trained together, ate together, and slept in the same rooms. IMG was my freedom.

Over the years, I lived in eight different dorms at IMG. At the end of every school year, I packed up my things and headed home for summer break. Then I returned in the fall to a new dorm and new roommates.

When I was thirteen, my new roommate was Sesil Karatantcheva. Sesil was a really good junior player, a Bulgarian phenom. In 2004, shortly after becoming my roommate, she won the Junior French Open at Roland-Garros. Sesil achieved a world number-one junior ranking that same year. When we first met, I didn't know where Bulgaria was. Sesil was very sweet, and we had fun together. She even taught me some Bulgarian phrases, ones that stuck with me later when I had a Bulgarian teammate in college.

Sesil came to IMG on a scholarship and was signed to IMG at the time. She was a couple of years older than me but still young and really good for her age. This was extremely motivating for me because I was still in Coach Jairo's group. In comparison, I didn't measure up. Sesil never let that impact how she treated me as a friend, which was rare because back then tennis people really treated you differently if you weren't highly ranked.

When Sesil was my roommate, I watched her practice with the best women's players. She was in Nick's pro girl group with Nicole Vaidišová, Alisa Kleybanova, and Sabine Lisicki, and I would watch the best male players practice too, guys like Philip Bester from Canada; Marcus Fugate from Rochester, New York (my hometown); Aljoscha Thron from Germany; Gastão Elias from Portugal; Filip Krajinović from Serbia; Kei Nishikori from Japan; and Holden Seguso, the son of Carling Bassett-Seguso and Robert Seguso, who played on tour.

I also watched Donald Young, who was number one in the world in ITF Juniors. Donald was a prominent tennis player and a good guy. Like me, he was a lefty. He was also the first Black American to be number one in the world in juniors. He was younger than the other star players, being born in 1989 versus 'eighty-seven, and I had a massive crush on him. Before I had the guts to tell my friends how I felt about him, I watched Donald practice, in awe of his skill. He was a lefty like me, and I wanted to see if I could learn anything from what he was doing. Donald always had the best style. Sponsored by Nike, he wore a hat turned to one side and diamond earrings. He followed a specific routine before every point, playing with his strings and turning his racket. He had a specific way of walking around the court.

I was super nervous around Donald, so after I told my friends Carling Seguso and Nicole Bartnik how I felt, they told him. We were kids at the time. A popular song was "You Don't Know My Name" by Alicia Keys. In the music video, Alicia works in a coffee shop. She has a crush on a guy who comes into the shop often, and she finally gets the courage to call him and ask him out over the phone.

When my friends told Donald how I felt, he told them to tell me to be like Alica Keys in that video. "Tell her to just come and talk to me," he said. Even though I was usually outgoing and social, I was super nervous and shy around Donald. I blushed and froze up. If you remember your first crush and the butterflies you got, you know exactly how I felt!

Being thirteen and with a huge crush, I had drawn a picture of Donald holding a trophy. I thought of giving it to him, but I didn't (whew). He was nice to me, and we had a pleasant conversation, but it didn't turn into anything. We did stay friends, though. He was a great guy, and his mom and coach, IIona, was also really nice. I'd see her on the campus every now and then. I think she was used to girls flocking around Donald because she was super serious, and she probably didn't want him to become distracted. Looking back I totally understand why. I wasn't allowed to date either, but for some reason, I had taken my shot. It wouldn't be the last time I took a chance to meet a boy I liked. Sometimes making the first move worked in my favor, but other times, I caught a guy off-guard. I think they were surprised to have a girl reach out to them like that, and sometimes it got weird. More on that later.

After IMG, Donald and I stayed in touch through social media. We'd also run into one another at tournaments, and I've been a huge supporter of his all these years. After all, we sort of grew up together and played in the same circles. I don't know if I ever told him he was my first crush (well, after Mark with a K from fifth grade), but he'd probably find that pretty funny.

My dad hired a private coach for me right away. In New York, I was a big fish in a little pond. At IMG, I was up against the best of the best from around the world. Group lessons and matches would improve my game, but to have any chance of playing at the highest level and getting to be in Percy's group, I needed much more personalized training.

My first private coach at IMG was Jimmy Nagelsen. My parents met him when they were buying the house near the school in the Palm Court neighborhood of El Con. Coach Jimmy lived a few houses down from us. He saw them moving in and introduced himself right away. His sister, Betsy Nagelsen McCormack, was a retired professional tennis player, and she was involved with IMG early on. Jimmy was a coach there and well-known around campus as someone who could develop younger students at lower levels who needed a lot of help to raise their game.

Jimmy had a vibrant personality. Sometimes he'd yell at me, even throw tennis balls at me. Not aggressively, but almost in a comical way. I laughed, but I also knew he was serious, and I needed to pay attention. I trained with him several days a week. Those months were among the toughest of my life. Jimmy not only did tennis training, but he had me in the gym with him and the handful of players he coached privately. We were a special group, and I attribute my six-pack abs to working with Jimmy. He had us doing so many ab exercises back then. I still remember some days when it would rain and he would take us all to this restaurant called Peaches, which was the cutest little breakfast spot in Bradenton, Florida. It was *our* spot. He was a regular, and the staff treated us so kindly. We trained so hard for so many hours, so when it rained, all of us celebrated. We knew for a brief moment we would get a break, just a couple of hours when we didn't need to worry about practice and we could go to Peaches to get breakfast.

I had come to IMG thinking I was special, but seeing the other prominent girls showed me how far I had to go. My confidence back then was nonexistent. No matter how hard I tried, I couldn't see myself ever getting into a group like Coach Percy's on my own. My parents knew how much I wanted it, but they reinforced daily the work it was going to take. I committed to trusting the training and the process, and Jimmy pushed me constantly, telling me to try harder and give it my all every lesson. He convinced me that I would improve by giving one hundred percent every time. So many tears shed on that court. I was really pushing myself. Pushing past limits that I had created in my mind.

This was so new to me. Playing in New York, I wasn't used to that physicality. Pushing myself every time I hit the court was a big adjustment, and an important one in my development as a player. Many days, I'd be in tears, but I'd push through, counting every tiny improvement as a win. You may be thinking, *How hard could it be?* Try running side to side hitting tennis balls and having to hit specific targets. And if you don't hit them, you have to keep doing the drills until you do. This is where the consistency and the fundamentals in my game were built. If I was going to play against these girls who "pushed" the ball, meaning they would not miss, I needed to be accurate, and I needed to be sure that I could last. Being that I was tall and skinny, I would want to set things up so I could end points by hitting a forehand to the right-handed person's backhand. But in order to get there, I would need to be consistent enough and not miss in the process. This was where all those hours of training would begin to pay off.

As tough as he was, Jimmy believed in me. He saw that I didn't believe in myself. He'd say, "Once you believe in yourself the way I believe in you, you'll be great." I wanted to believe, but the light at the end of the tunnel seemed so far away. It seemed like it would never happen. Every day I saw the other girls playing in Percy's group and in Nick's group, practicing, and they hit the ball so cleanly. They got so much attention and praise. They had the focus and gaze of Nick and Gabriel Jaramillo. I wanted, just once, for them to notice me.

Once a player got to a certain level, they hired a different coach.

I always wondered if that bothered Jimmy. He worked so hard to help players improve, and then they moved on. I never forgot my roots and where I came from. My time with Jimmy really shaped my experience. I had a whole team of coaches to improve my game. Jimmy was a major piece of that puzzle, but he wasn't the only one.

COACH LANCE

While I was still hitting with Jimmy, I also began playing with another coach, Lance Luciani. Coach Lance had his own program inside IMG called Strategy Zone that focused on specific shots and strategies. Lance was knowledgeable about cameras and video, and he knew how to record every aspect of a player's strokes to see exactly what they were doing. He was instrumental in teaching my dad how to use a contraption that allowed you to put a video camera on top of a pole that could be placed on the fence of any tennis court. This was a game changer because it allowed every match I played to be recorded and analyzed. Back then this was common practice in sports like football and basketball, but in tennis, it was new and state of the art. Working with Lance opened me up to other coaches who worked with him, including Margie Zesinger, a tall blonde coach who commanded every room she walked into. Margie had been personally mentored by Nick Bollettieri. He took a liking to her and saw her potential as a leader at the Academy. Margie's confidence and energy attracted me to her. I loved my lessons with her, partly because, at five feet ten inches, she was tall like me. At five feet nine inches at that time, I could look her eye to eye. I was still skinny and lanky, though, barely a hundred pounds. She was a huge role model for me.

Margie really helped me explode into the balls I hit and not be afraid to take risks with my shots. She pushed me to hit swing volleys and be aggressive. She was patient with me and an amazing mentor on and off the court.

Margie stayed at IMG all these years and is still there today. Throughout her career, she poured her heart into developing young girls with big dreams, coaching top-ten world-ranked juniors—players who went on to win Eddie Herr, the Orange Bowl, and Junior Grand Slam titles. I watched her guide countless girls through the leap from juniors to the pros, helping them earn their first professional titles and reach career-high WTA rankings. She also shaped NCAA Division I champions, teaching them how to compete at the highest levels with passion and gusto.

Margie didn't just coach on the ITF Pro Circuit and WTA Tour—she lived the journey alongside her players. She spent years at USTA and Team USA national camps working with the best American juniors and giving them the belief that they belonged on the world stage. Today, she's the head of female tennis at IMG. Everything goes through her, and there couldn't be a better person to keep Nick's legacy going.

And for me, Margie's impact was immense. She believed in me early on, and years later, she invited me back to IMG to speak to the female program—a full-circle moment I'll always treasure. I'm deeply grateful for her guidance and for the connection we built. As new moms, we also shared so many amazing moments as we navigated unfamiliar territory with our young boys.

3

DESTINED FOR TENNIS

I didn't grow up in Rochester proper but in the city's largest suburb, a town called Greece. Like Rochester, Greece is usually cold. Not just cold but frigid. The lake-effect snow is a constant, and I wasn't made for it.

The few warm months are heavenly, and those are where my earliest memories lie—springtime at Sawyer Park in Greece. I still remember playing with tennis balls at the Athena High School tennis courts. My parents were playing tennis, or my dad was hitting balls against an enormous wall. I was surrounded by grass and flowers. Everything smelled nice, and other than the rhythmic whack of my parents' rackets, it was quiet. There was no one else there—just the three of us. I must have been just two years old because by the time I was three, they had me in tennis lessons.

I started training at the Midtown Athletic Club. Several times a week for seven years, I practiced, played, and trained at the club. Mom drove me there when I was little and later, when I attended Montessori preschool.

In preschool, I struggled with scissors. They didn't feel right in my hand. While the other kids seemed to use them with ease, I couldn't get them to work properly. The teacher saw me fumbling and gave me a different pair of scissors. They worked perfectly! That was when I realized I was left-handed.

Parents often push their "lefty" kids to abandon their left-handedness in favor of right-hand dominance. But left-handed people think differently, often to their advantage. Evidence shows left-handed people tend to use both sides of their brains to handle tasks typically assigned to one side or the other.

My parents didn't discourage my left-handedness. They were proud of my differences and recognized this particular uniqueness came with advantages, specifically in tennis. For example, lefties are better at visual and spatial processing. Later, as I played more tennis, I came to appreciate the distinction. (My favorite uncle, my dad's older brother Uncle Terry, is also left-handed. We're both lefties and have flat feet.)

From preschool, I went on to Allendale Columbia Elementary, and my mother continued picking me up after school and dropping me off at the tennis club. My routine wasn't like the other kids'. They went home and relaxed with their families or played with their friends. I, on the other hand, was always heading to and from practice. Back then, practice was up to two hours long.

We lived in a four-bedroom, two-and-a-half-bath house in a middle-class neighborhood. I saw families outside together when I rode my bike, but I rarely interacted with them. We were one of the only Black families on the block, from my memory. There are a lot of white people in Rochester. I had a couple of neighborhood friends I was allowed to play with if they came over to our backyard. My parents didn't let me wander too far, but on a bike, I could go up and down the street if I was still in their view. This was before phones and air tagging kids, so you had to have enough trust that your kid wouldn't go too far.

My mom was thirty-six and Dad was thirty-four when they had me. It took my mother a couple of years to get pregnant. I know my parents wanted to be established financially and settled in their careers before having children. I can relate to this now; since becoming a parent, I've realized that being a parent is not easy. I always grew up wanting siblings, but that was a hard no conversation ender. It was just me, myself, and I. Looking back, I understand now, as a mom. It's a lot, and my parents did so much for me that they wouldn't have been able to do it if I wasn't alone.

We were a true family unit. If my dad needed something from Home Depot or Best Buy, we all went. It wasn't as if he couldn't manage these trips alone. That was just how we operated. My dad checked the new releases at Best Buy on Saturdays and Sundays. He had the largest collection of VHS tapes and then, later, DVDs. He had thousands of them. This was before streaming and having everything at your fingertips. My dad's collection speaks to his passion for electronics, technology, and always being ahead of his time. My parents are baby boomers, and music was super important to them. I knew all the hit music from the 1970s and '80s because it was what they always played. The music library in my head is like that of a sixty-year-old, and people are always shocked that I can sing, word for word, songs by Earth, Wind & Fire and Prince.

My mother's and father's parents, brothers, sisters, nieces, and nephews didn't live close by, so it was always just the three of us. We visited my grandparents, aunts, uncles, and cousins twice a year. My Aunt Sharon was a favorite. Growing up, I always remember bonding with her. She was tall like me, beautiful, and always knew what she wanted. She had impeccable style and the trendiest haircuts. When she walked into a room, everyone noticed. Whenever I saw her, I always thought, *I can't wait to get older so I can be like her.* Today, as the ex-wife of my dad's brother Terry, Sharon is a successful multimillion-dollar real estate agent in Jacksonville. Like my father, she knew how to achieve success against all odds.

Uncle Terry, a retired regional vice president of an automotive finance corporation, was also someone I looked up to. Like Aunt Sharon, he also exudes success. In my childhood, my aunt and uncle moved several times, all for promotions my uncle earned in his executive career. I always thought it was so cool because each move meant a new house, and each one was bigger and more lavish. I never fully understood what they did for a living until later, but I knew I was super excited when they finally moved to Jacksonville, Florida, after years of moving around the Midwest. My dad is seven years younger than Uncle Terry and always looked up to him. My dad was the youngest, and Uncle Terry was the oldest.

Mom and Dad rarely went on dates, from what I can remember. I can count on one hand the number of times they hired a babysitter to stay with me. They didn't go out with friends much either. There were no "nights out with the guys" or "girls' days out." I think this was because they really loved being around each other and me. But looking back, I'm surprised they didn't maintain much of a social life after having a child. I think this was also because my parents had to do so many work dinners and other functions; they didn't really want to be away from home if they didn't have to. My dad is more of a homebody than my mom, but my dad made the home fun with TVs everywhere with movies and sports always playing.

My mother, Norma Iris Mills, was born in Bayamon, Puerto Rico, in the mid-1950s. Her mom, my abuela or, as they called her, Ma, moved them to Hoboken, New Jersey, in 1957. There, my abuela met a taxi driver who used to take her and her daughter, my mother, to and from work every day. He had recently become a widower with five children. An arrangement was made for my grandmother and my toddler mother to move into his two-bedroom apartment and help take care of his kids. Together, my abuela and the taxi driver had eight more children. Throughout the years, seven or eight children at a time lived with them in that tiny two-bedroom apartment.

Mom grew up thinking that the taxi driver, who they all called Pops, was her father. Years later, after noticing there was no surname listed on her birth certificate, which was needed in order for her to get her first passport, she did some investigating and realized she had a different father from her siblings. It wasn't until she was thirty-five that she finally met her biological dad in Bayamon, Puerto Rico. This opened her up to a whole side of her family that she didn't know she had. Her dad, Benjamin Cabrera, never had any more kids. He lived into his nineties.

My mother was the first person in her family to go to college and graduate. She met my dad during summer school of her sophomore year in the 1970s. Mom was a couple of years older than Dad. They were in the same year in college because her mom didn't realize they had to put her in kindergarten when she was five, so she started two years late. Once in college, she got a part-time job at the school cafeteria and after that at the college day care center where the professors dropped off their kids. After my parents got together, my dad helped my mom get a job with him at a Sears department store. He also helped her get a job at the college's sports arena as an usher at the games. My dad worked three jobs, all while going to school. He jokes that he made more money in college than his parents did at the time. My dad got my mom into the mindset of working, and she also picked up jobs in college. They moved in together and have been together ever since. Once they graduated, she worked at a construction site, and then when my father moved from doing claims and underwriting into opening his own insurance agency, she began working with him. Some years later, Dad helped her set up her own insurance agency that was called Insurance Direct, and they became competitors. Mom ran her business for ten years until she sold it to move to Florida.

My mother worked a lot of weekends. I watched both my parents work seven days a week. There were no days off, just days with less work than other days. She'd take me into the office with her, and it would be just the two of us. I went to work with my dad occasionally, too, but mostly with Mom. For my parents, work wasn't a place you went to between all the things you wanted to do. It was a natural way of life. I got the sense that they wanted to be there—like they enjoyed working, or, correction, maybe they didn't *enjoy* working, but as two minorities trying to make it in the '90s, I'm sure they realized they had to work hard to be successful. I adopted the same ethic very early on.

My mother is one hundred percent Puerto Rican. Even though people see me as Black or as half Black and half white, I always correct them, saying, "I'm half Puerto Rican and half Black."

I got my height from my dad. My mom is just five feet tall, a petite woman. She's also the sweetest, most caring person you'd ever want to meet. One of her sisters, Chillie, was born with a severe case of multiple sclerosis and meningitis, and my mom grew up watching her mother take care of her. Chillie couldn't eat the way her siblings did; she took her food through a tube. She couldn't walk and couldn't talk either, using only facial expressions to communicate her feelings. But she was an extremely happy person. I believe that experience shaped my mom's caring side and taught her to be grateful for everything she had, including the ability to feed herself and walk on her own. Having such a severely handicapped family member shaped the way my mom's side of the family views life and the world.

Mom was so fortunate to stay home with me for the first three years of my life, and our days were filled with visits to parks and museums and special events like the Annual Lilac Festival. After decades, I still can't forget the scent of all those flowers. She filled our days with activities, exploring all around Rochester, New York. We went to Charlotte Beach and went bike riding all around.

My mother loved music. She listened to the salsa singer Celia Cruz. Both of my parents listened to a lot of 1970s and '80s music. They were big on Motown, and I grew up listening to Earth, Wind & Fire, Lionel Richie, Sly and the Family Stone, Fleetwood Mac, Michael Jackson, and Prince. Basically, anybody Quincy Jones worked with I knew, and if it was '80s music, I knew every word.

Though all four of my grandparents were pretty religious, neither of my parents leaned into any one belief. We didn't go to church except occasionally on a holiday. We always celebrated the Christian holidays of Christmas and Easter. I wasn't baptized, and religion was not a major part of my upbringing. I think that was because my parents were forced into religion by their parents, so they pushed against those teachings. While I never discovered for sure, I believe my parents, like me, are spiritual people who just don't follow specific religious rules.

My mother's first language was Spanish, or really "Spanglish," but she didn't speak it to me often around the house. I think this was how she was raised after moving to New Jersey from Puerto Rico. Her family wanted to fit in with the neighborhood, and that meant speaking English. Back then, the world was more racist than today and being different brought about unnecessary attention and bullying. Thinking of how much of a melting pot New Jersey and New York are, I was surprised to hear this, but I can understand wanting to fit in and just be "American." Puerto Ricans *are* Americans, but you know what I mean. I think this is one of the major reasons so many Puerto Ricans in the USA lose their language. Unlike people from the Dominican Republic, Cuba, and other Latin American island countries, where people move to America, keep the language going, and pass it down, it's extremely common to know Puerto Ricans whose grandparents speak Spanish, but their kids and grandkids only know English, so the language dies.

When I was young, the only time I heard Mom speak her native language was when she was on the phone with my abuela, who didn't speak English very well, or when she was surrounded by her uncles and aunts, and even then, only if they initiated it. She'd talk in Spanglish—a combination of the two languages—so I could sometimes follow along, but it was mostly gibberish to my ears. I kind of regret that because if she had spoken Spanish around me when I was a baby, I would have picked it up sooner instead of learning it on my own later in life through songs, movies, and a burning desire to find my culture.

My mom spoke Spanish more often when I started traveling

for tennis tournaments. Many countries we visited were primarily Spanish-speaking, so her bilingualism came in handy. We spent a lot of time in Mexico, and also in Colombia and other South American countries. As a teenager, I became obsessed with learning Spanish and, later, Portuguese. I translated song lyrics to help me memorize the words and forced myself to use different languages with native speakers at tennis tournaments. My Spanish today is not perfect, but I'm proud to understand ninety percent of what is spoken to me, and I can speak about seventy percent fluently. My writing is the strongest. I've also made the conscious decision to speak to my son, Otto, in only Spanish as much as possible, even though my grammar isn't perfect. He is in a bilingual school, and I want him to still connect his mom with Spanish since he is one-quarter Puerto Rican.

Mom was (and still is) a superb cook. She made Pureto Rican meals with rice and beans. We had my mom's traditional meals along with typical American meals that included steak, pork chops, chicken, and a lot of vegetables. She cooked every meal for the family—breakfast, lunch, and dinner. She also did most of the housework. My parents were traditional in that sense. Because their insurance agency was doing so well, my mom was fortunate enough to stay at home with me for my first three years of life. I always said if I had a baby I wanted to be able to do the same because I spent so many amazing moments with my mom during those three years. Nothing against day care or getting a nanny; I just was so lucky to have a mom who was really loving and caring, and she appeared to really be enjoying being a new mom. Before those three years, my parents were starting a new life in a new city with brand-new jobs. Mom was not able to transfer her current job, so she went to work for my dad. They worked together up until the time I was born. They did what worked best for them.

Mom always did breakfast, and they were off to work. Lunches and dinners depended on the work schedule that day. Most lunches were in the office around clients and work. Dinners were simple and again around work schedules. They were trying to build a business pretty much from scratch, so that took all their time. Mom made dinner after work when dad had appointments. She also worked full time in the office, and most times when they left together, they picked up dinner to go. Mom enjoyed working in the office with the staff and the customers. I remember thinking that I didn't want a traditional, gender-specific role when I grew up and got married. I wanted to share all the responsibilities with my partner. I don't know why I wanted this so much. So many girls are raised to become good wives and cook, clean, and find a strong man to take care of them and the household. A man who will provide and protect. With my intense sports background, this was not my upbringing at all. My parents only focused on how I could be the best version of me at all times and never settle for mediocrity.

I think my mom left most of the business decisions to my father because she trusted his sense of business. In that way, their roles were extremely old-fashioned. I always wondered what she would have been like if she had taken on a more active role in that part of their relationship. I think part of her behavior was due to her upbringing and how my father helped to change her life for the better. When she met him, she was making up a semester in summer school. My father, meanwhile, was from a very stable family. He was going to college while holding down three part-time jobs. Getting together with my dad elevated her life in many ways, and I think she was always grateful for that. To this day, they operate as a unit, doing everything together. You rarely see them apart, and they truly come as a package deal. If they had read *The five Love Languages: The Secret to Love that Lasts* by Dr. Gary Chapman back then, their strongest languages would have been "quality time" and "acts of service." That describes them both to a T. They're not into gift-giving or celebrations. We never made a big deal out of holidays or even celebrated birthdays. I rarely heard them use any words of affirmation. They showed love through time and acts of service.

My parents' relationship works extremely well for them, but it was not a life I wanted for myself. I always wanted an equal partnership where my partner and I contributed not only financially but in every other way. I wanted an equal say in everything. Being old school or having a traditional marriage was way more common back then, and honestly, with the rate of divorce being sixty percent, my parents are one of the few examples I have in my life of couples that are still married.

I don't think my attitude around gender roles was based solely on my generation. Plenty of girls—especially women I met in college—were eager to get married so they could stay home and be taken care of. They didn't even want to contribute financially like my mom did by working for herself or working with my dad. They wanted to be fully supported. To me, full support meant full control, and I wanted no part of that. I've always wanted to be in control of my life and my destiny and not hand that power over to anyone else.

Mom took care of the house. Dad took care of the cars and made sure the bills got paid. My father, Barion Mills Jr, was born in Frankfurt, Germany, in 1957. A military brat, his family lived in Thailand for several years while he attended elementary school. Dad was the youngest of three. His middle sister, Beverly, who was like my grandmother's twin, passed away in her thirties from a medical condition she'd dealt with her whole life. I never met her because she passed away before I was born. My dad, being the youngest, always had his sister and brother to look up to. I'm sure he got a different version of my grandparents than they did, since back then my grandma had my Uncle Terry as a late teenager, but that was the norm in the 1950s and '60s.

At six feet one, my father, a light-skinned Black man, had an extreme presence when he walked into a room. He had a look and a tone that let you know he wasn't fooling around, but at any moment, he could smile and be the most inviting, friendly person. Dad had certain expectations, and he expected you to follow his rules. He didn't yell often. I can count on one hand the number of times he raised his voice at me. I think I got spanked four or five times in my whole childhood. I didn't need the threat of being yelled at or spanked to stay in line. If I could sum up Dad in two words, those words would be "prepared" and "organized." He has a process for just about everything. He has files and folders for everything else.

My father was always obsessed with sports and electronics. Before smartphones, he carried a portable TV everywhere so he wouldn't miss a game, especially football and basketball. Dad also obsessed over tennis. No matter what he was doing, there was always a TV on in the background. In our house's basement, there was a big-screen television with three smaller TVs stacked one on top of the other. This was before picture-in-picture.

We had at least one TV in every room. I thought this was normal until I visited other people's homes where there was just one TV in the entire house. Listening to one thing while doing something else was important for my dad. At dinner, he'd have an earpiece in, and he'd be listening to sports or talking to someone about business. To this day, I don't know how my father can keep track of scores and talk about work at the same time.

Business was another obsession for my father. He worked for a large corporation and was very successful, one of the top five sales agents in the country for State Farm Insurance, the country's largest auto insurer. Dad was the company's number-one agent for two years at one point. He wrote a book called *Stress-Free Success*. He also traveled and gave speeches.

My dad didn't shield me from Black culture, but it wasn't a big part of our lives either. We listened to Black music from the 1970s and '80s, but we didn't speak Black slang or listen to current music from Black culture. Because of his work, and perhaps how he was raised, my father was part of a corporate, white world, and he knew how to fit in.

My father is competitive and very strict. Not surprisingly, growing up in a military family and a regimented, structured environment. He claims he's not as strict as his own dad, but until I was twelve, my bedtime was seven o'clock. So no sleepovers. Nothing that might put me out of my dad's sight and potentially at risk.

I was nervous around my father when I was young. He'd yell at me for things that I thought were unimportant, like standing a certain way or accidentally dropping something. He'd get upset with me when I lost a game. I thought his way was the only way and that I was imperfect. As I got older, I realized there were ten different ways to slice bread, not just Dad's way. I also understood his way of thinking, and that nervousness dissipated.

I learned a lot from my dad. My discipline, work ethic, and networking skills are all because of him. He and my mother took me along on trips to Europe when I was young, an ambassador travel trip to Spain he'd earned through the success of his agency, where I was the only kid. It was normal for me to sit at a table with ten adults, entertaining myself with a coloring book and pretending not to "eavesdrop" while secretly listening to their conversations.

My parents never baby-talked to me. They treated me like an adult. I've read theories about only children being naturally more mature, in part because they don't have siblings to act like children with, and I don't know if that's true, but I felt like an adult. I was still a kid in many ways, too, though. I played with toys, but in my room, by myself. I stayed out of trouble. Following rules was ingrained in me early on, and I didn't want to cross Dad, so I did what I was supposed to do.

Dad worked days, nights, and weekends. He'd take me to his office, which was much bigger than my mother's. He had about twenty-five people working for him, and they were all very nice to me. I hung out in the break room and read the posters, checked out the pamphlets.

My father never said he wanted a boy instead of me, a girl, but I sensed it. I believe he wanted a son who could do all the things he wanted for himself. Dad was an athlete in school, playing football and basketball. When he tore up his leg during a football game in his senior year of high school, scouts stopped looking at him for a scholarship.

He made the football team as a walk-on at Rutgers University, where he majored in communications, but at the same time, he was working three part-time jobs. Dad worked as an orderly at a hospital and an usher at the NBA's New Jersey Nets games. He also worked in the parts and service area at Sears, and he was a volunteer teacher's assistant in the communications department at Rutgers.

He ended up quitting the team to focus on making money. While he was in college, my father paid for his own tuition and a new car. After his first year, he also paid for an off-campus apartment for himself and my mother. My mother worked too. She and my father were ushers at Nets and Rutgers basketball games. They also did data entry for Sears and worked at other part-time jobs.

Dad loved playing tennis and watching other players. He was an avid spectator and knew everything about the sport. He and my mother had planned to name me Gabriela, after the great Gabriela Sabatini. They switched to Danielle at the last minute.

If I had been a boy, my father probably would have pushed me into baseball or basketball. He put me in tennis because he believed I could make the most money as an individual player rather than as part of a team. At that time, tennis was the highest-paying female professional sport. In my father's eyes, tennis was my key to success, and my success was everything to my parents. Dad loved sports, but he may have loved money—and the security and control that comes with it—even more.

IT WAS ALWAYS GOING TO BE TENNIS

As a kid growing up in New York, I was super skinny, and very tall for my age. At five feet seven and ninety-seven pounds, I was the tallest and thinnest girl in the class. I wore pink glasses.

Boys didn't pay attention to me. I had a crush on one boy, Mark (with a *k*, versus Marc with a *c*, another boy in the class). He was every fifth grader's crush; with blond hair and light-blue eyes, he was so cute, but he would look at me with empty eyes, as if he were looking through me. I wasn't one of the cool kids who played soccer. I played once, but I missed a kick, and everyone saw. I thought I would die of embarrassment. None of that helped my confidence.

I stood out for all the wrong reasons, including being the only girl who played tennis. I did everything I could to fit in, even getting my hair straightened. Back then, I just wanted to be like everyone else. I'd think, *Why can't I play soccer? Why can't I go to other girls' houses? Have sleepovers?* But none of that was allowed.

Tennis was allowed, so I made it my life. I lived for practice, but not the matches. The fear of losing and of how my parents would react to a loss was painful. My first tournament ended with a six-o, six-o loss. My dad was really upset, and I hated seeing him like that. I knew I had tried my best, and I wanted that to be good enough. But his disappointment made me feel ashamed. After that, I never wanted to lose again.

Sometimes I'd be playing well and on track for a win when the fear of losing would interrupt my flow and I'd choke. Those were the games that upset me the most because I knew that physically, I should have won. I needed to tackle the mental game. That would come later.

Thankfully, I didn't lose often. Few girls competed in the Western New York region, so the draws were small. I might have to win only two matches to win the whole tournament. In other regions, girls had to win six or seven. That advantage improved my ranking quickly. Unfortunately, it also presented me with a false reality. I probably thought I was better than I was. IMG was my wake-up call.

My parents did the best they could for me, better than most parents. In many ways, I was extremely lucky. They supported me and had the best intentions. They wanted me to have a good life—to have everything. At the time, I didn't understand that. Later, when I was an adult and a parent, it made more sense. Though I wouldn't raise my own child exactly like they raised me, many of their lessons became a part of who I am as a person and a parent.

For elementary school, I went to Allendale Columbia, a prestigious, private K–twelve school in nearby Pittsburgh, another suburb of Rochester. It took thirty-five minutes to get to school by bus, including transferring buses at a school stop, and I spent all that time doing my homework.

The classrooms were small, and the academic standards were high. Classes were a mix of ten or twelve boys and girls from affluent families, and we split into two groups of five or six kids for lessons. To teachers, I was known as "the good student who can't focus." I always had my hand up, asking or answering questions. I'd start a problem and move to the next one without finishing the first one. My progress reports told the same story over and over: *Danielle needs to listen and pay attention in class. She needs to focus.*

What I remember most about school is being excited to be around other people. I spent so much time alone or with my parents that going to school and being around other children felt like freedom. We wore uniforms, so you couldn't tell which kids' parents spent the most money on clothes. I never experienced or witnessed bullying or any of the other negative behaviors that were common in public schools. A few kids had ADHD or other learning challenges. The school accommodated them, and no one treated them differently from anyone else. At school, I did my best to blend in. I was friendly and helpful. If I saw someone sitting alone in the cafeteria, I'd sit with them. That part of me comes from my mother. She always makes people feel welcome and included.

I was one of just two Black girls in the elementary school. The other girl was Andria Boyde Langston. Her dad owned a radio station, 104 WDKX, and I just remember how cool that was. Andria was my first best friend at the school. Today, she's a successful actress starring in movies and running her own podcast. Andria and I had similar interests. She was an Aries, like me, and we were born just a few days apart. We bonded over having ethnic hair, which was often the topic of conversation in our class. We didn't stay in touch as well after elementary school, but we're supportive of one another's careers, and it's super cool to see two Black girls from Rochester, New York, doing big things in the world.

The kids I knew from school didn't live nearby, and none of them played tennis, so there were no opportunities for me to interact with them outside of school. Secretly, I wanted to play soccer like they did, but that wasn't in the cards. Mom and Dad wanted a tennis player.

On days when I didn't have tennis practice, I went to an after-school program at the YMCA. I had a Game Boy, and I got into video games and Pokémon. The Game Boy came from my dad. He introduced me to electronics, and every year they'd get me a new gaming system to play with. I played alone at home and after school. My dad didn't play with me, but I think he bought me things like this because he didn't have them when he was a kid. The downside of all the electronics was that they took me away from reading. I had been an avid reader, but once I got hooked on electronics, it was tough to go back to reading.

I started competing in tournaments when I was seven. Because the population was limited, the draws were small. I could win a match or two and take the whole tournament. This gave me a state ranking. While that looked good on paper, it gave me a false sense of my skill. It wasn't until I moved to Florida and competed against girls from across the country and around the world that I realized I had been a big fish in a small pond.

In competition, I realized the benefits of being a lefty. When a left-handed player hits a tennis ball, it spins in the opposite direction of a right-handed player. Returning a lefty's serve or hit is unusual for players, and thus more challenging. Of course, playing against lefties is also more difficult for left-handed players, but two lefties rarely face one another on the court.

My parents hired my first tennis coach, Ron Dyson, when I was about five or six. He and I worked together almost every day. Before that, I had practiced in group clinics with other little kids. I needed individual instruction because of the nature of the sport. I needed one-on-one time. I needed to focus on technique to get really good. I couldn't do that in a group.

I loved my lessons, and I loved practicing. The workouts were fun. I did not like the matches. I didn't enjoy the competition. Mostly, I didn't like the thought of not winning. That made me nervous. I didn't want to disappoint my father, and I knew he wouldn't be happy unless I won every match, every tournament.

As disappointed as my father was over a loss, his reaction to wins was neutral. I wasn't peppered with lots of praise. He recognized my wins but then followed up the acknowledgment with details on what I did wrong and what I needed to do the next time to play better. I think this comes from his perpetual desire to push me to be my best. There was *always* room for improvement. Dad had very high expectations, and nothing was ever good enough, it seemed. Looking back, I appreciate this because it truly has allowed me to not look at anything average and accept it. I must strive for the best at all times with anything I focus on.

The closest I ever came to meeting his expectations was winning a tournament. I couldn't imagine any greater success. In tennis, there is only one winner. That person has achieved perfection. I wanted to be perfect.

4

THE TRAINING GROUND

On my first day at the Academy, after the selection process, each coach took their respective group aside to explain how they'd work together. Coach Jairo told us he'd be our head coach, and we'd be spending time with him every day. Before practice, we were to check out the board by the cafeteria to see which court we were on. The academy had about fifty courts, so knowing where to go and how to get there was important. It could take a while to get across the campus and be on time, and punctuality was critical. I'd check the board every night to see if I could make the next day's practice on time on foot or if I'd need to find transportation. If morning practice was at the Academy Park courts, I'd set my alarm to get up earlier and give myself more time. There were consequences for being late.

Training comprised drills and play. We worked on the main tennis shots—forehand, backhand, serve, overhead, slice, and drop shot—individually and in combinations. The coach had a shopping cart of tennis balls, each one stamped *Penn: the ball sponsor of IMG.* Coach Jairo stood on the other side of the net and threw these balls at players, one after another. We took short breaks to pick up all the balls and put them back in the cart. Then we played against each other, testing the skills we practiced in the drills.

Getting stuck in the next-to-worst skill level group was a rude awakening for me, and more so for my dad. Within days, he set me up with individual private coaching. He looked over my tennis and academics schedule and filled any free time with private lessons. Monday through Friday, I'd go from team training and practice to a private lesson, then academics followed by another private lesson.

There was a hierarchy among the students and their parents. I felt it, and I know my dad felt it too. If we were going to gain respect in that environment, I had to level up quickly and earn my way into a higher group of players. The pressure was on, and I was on board with it.

At first, I didn't understand how crazy my schedule would be. I was constantly training and playing. It was a lot for a kid my age, but I had to stick with it to improve. That meant a lot of early mornings and late evenings, week after week and month after month.

My father signed me up for tournaments every weekend. If I did well in competition, that meant my Monday through Friday training had paid off. If I did poorly, I would have to spend the next week working on whatever weak skills had caused my defeat.

The tournaments started right away. I competed in the lowest-level local USTA events. If we couldn't find a tournament outside the Academy, I played in an IMG tournament called a Grand Prix. These were scheduled about once a month, and students competed in a draw by age range, not by group and skill level. So one day I might compete against someone in my own group, and the next time, I'd be playing against a much better player in Coach Percy's group.

The practice, lessons, and playing were nonstop. If I did well on the weekend, I'd finish two full matches in a day. It was a lot. My day started at five in the morning, five fifteen if I could afford to sleep in. I'd have my clothes laid out so I could get dressed quickly, then head to the cafeteria. At first, I walked to the courts, but once

I realized how far some of them were, I got a Razor scooter. Physical conditioning started at six, followed by tennis practice with my group from seven to nine. We did drills and worked on shots and other aspects of the game.

Then we'd spend an hour and a half playing challenge matches against other groups within a level or two of ours. I always wanted to play better players, not only to improve my game but because the potential for losing to a player in a lower group was frightening. We were expected to beat those players. Of course, it felt great to beat a better player. But the fear of losing to a worse player added a lot of pressure. It happened, though. I could have a bad day, and they could have a good one, or vice versa. The uncertainty was mentally challenging.

At ten thirty, I did more physical conditioning. This was different from the earlier session, which was more of a warmup. For an hour, we hit the gym, and then the field, for weightlifting, agility and balance training, and band work. The exercises were all specific to tennis.

After that training, it was time for mental conditioning, which was exercises to sharpen my mindset. Those lessons included visualization, where I'd close my eyes, envision myself playing tennis, and imagine every detail of the game. This was mental preparation so that when I played a real game, I'd feel more comfortable and confident—as if I'd already been there.

We did a lot of routine building too. These are repeatable habits you build into your game. For example, before serving, a player could bounce the ball three times, touch their racket strings, bounce the ball one more time, and then serve. After the point is over, they could turn and walk to the backdrop of the court, look at their strings, say something to themselves, take six breaths, then walk back up to the line. Routines help keep a player's mind free of distractions and focused on the game.

Onlookers often notice only the physicality of the sport, but tennis is a very mental game. It's you versus the opponent. No team to rely on, or blame, when you fail. Negative mindsets lose games. If an opponent gets in your head, you lose focus. When your mind goes in that direction, you can "spiral out" or "flame out," "choke," and, ultimately, lose.

This happens when you lose consecutive points. You could lose a point, leading to losing four points, then losing the entire game. Lose too many games and lose the match. The momentum toward winning or losing can shift quickly, so keeping focused, positive, and in a winning state of mind is imperative.

Staying focused on yourself and the game is the toughest part of playing tennis. You have to stay in the present, think about your foot placement and what you are doing at each moment. Not what you did five seconds ago or what you will do if you win or lose. It's so easy to imagine what will happen if you get the next point and you win the game and the whole match, and then your life changes. While you're having that thought, you make a major mistake that takes all that future away from you, sending you into a downward spiral. You can't let your mind wander, even for a second.

When things go wrong, no one is in your mind with you. No one else knows what you're thinking. They just see you miss a shot. So you suffer in that moment alone. The time you spend in your head can get very lonely. It can show on your face, which you can't hide. It's a hard concept to explain to anyone who hasn't played.

Even golfers—who, like tennis players, also play individually rather than on a team—don't have a true opponent on the course. They play against the golf course, hoping someone else doesn't play against it better. They take time between strokes, whereas in tennis, you don't have that luxury. There is no countdown clock, so you can't ride the clock to a win, like in football. The game can shift in or out of your favor any second. A match can last one hour. It can last six hours. The players are on the court for the duration, never knowing how long the game will last.

You only get so many seconds after a point, and if you take too long, the umpire can take a point away from you. You have to move at the pace of the server. If you have a fast server and it's hot out, you struggle to keep up without overheating or getting worn out. Maybe boxers experience similar thoughts and feelings as tennis players, constantly facing an opponent. In tennis, you're fighting your opponent, the elements, and whatever's going on inside your head. And trying to get your body to respond in the best way possible every single second. Every sport has its individual challenges, but tennis, I believe, above all other sports, is one of the toughest sports mentally.

At IMG, Dad started video recording my matches. Filming other sports like football and basketball and then reviewing the tape was a normal part of those sports. You watched the video to see what a player did right and what they did wrong, and then determine what they had to change to do better. After every loss, I had to sit with my parents and review the entire recorded game, dissecting my performance point by point. On the bright side, those videos showed me where I needed to improve. However, as a kid who'd just lost a tennis match, the last thing I wanted to do was spend hours reviewing the whole nightmare and being reminded of everything I did wrong point by point. Looking back, this process we took after every match allowed me the skill to do post-game interviews and never get baffled by questions reporters asked. It also allowed me to have good answers to future coaches when they would grill me after a loss.

Pre-adolescent girls struggle with confidence and self-esteem. Imagine the added pressure, knowing people are always watching to see how you react to everything and everyone around you. At IMG, girls had meltdowns. They'd just fall apart during a game, crying on the court. Parents and coaches intervened to calm them.

The flip side of the individuality and accompanying loneliness of tennis are the wins. When you win at tennis, it's all you. Sure, you can thank your coach and your parents, but you are the one out there on the court doing the actual work. It feels good to win, taking in all the praise and the accolades. Unlike sports like football, where you wear a helmet, tennis players are out there bare faced for the world to see.

When I was growing up, tennis was its own little universe. A court, a ball, a racket, and a set of rules that seemed complicated until you lived inside them long enough that they became second nature. Whenever I explain the game to people who didn't grow up in it, I try to break it down the same way it was taught to me as a kid—simple, honest, and rooted in the rhythm of the sport.

At its core, tennis is a battle of consistency and control. Two players stand on opposite sides of a long rectangular court with a net stretched across the middle. In singles, it's just you and one opponent. In doubles, it's two players on each side, covering a wider court and relying on communication, trust, and timing.

Singles feels like a personal test. Doubles feels like a partnership. Both reveal who you are under pressure.

Every point starts with a player standing behind the baseline and tossing the ball into the air, serving it diagonally into the opposite service box. The player gets two chances to get the serve in. After that, it becomes a rally—a back-and-forth exchange where each player tries to outlast the other.

The rules are simple: the ball must clear the net and land inside the lines; the other player gets one bounce only, and if the ball lands outside the lines, hits the net, or bounces twice, the point is over.

Doubles is played similarly but with expanded sidelines, so there's more court to cover, more angles to protect, and more strategy built around teamwork. A great doubles team moves like one player with four legs and two rackets.

Tennis has a scoring system all its own—something that confuses almost everyone the first time they heard it, including me.

Instead of one, two, three, four, tennis uses love (zero), fifteen, thirty, forty, and game. If both players reach forty, it's called deuce, and you must win two points in a row—first advantage, then game. When everything else is even, the system rewards nerve and focus. Some of the most defining moments in my life happened at deuce, when every muscle in my body felt electric because everything was on the line.

Tennis is structured in layers: (one) win enough points to take a game; (two) win enough games (usually six, as long as you're ahead by two) to claim a set; and (three) win enough sets to win the match. Most men's and women's tennis around the world is played as best two out of three sets, but the Grand Slams—the biggest tournaments—are different: men play best three out of five sets, and women always play best two out of three at every event, including the Slams.

That difference makes men's matches in majors feel like marathons—physical and emotional tests that can go on longer than four or even five hours. Women's matches, though shorter on paper, are just as intense. Every point matters because there's less room to recover. Both formats demand their own kind of toughness.

Singles and doubles are two versions of the same truth. Singles is solitary, with you against someone else's game plan, someone else's endurance, someone else's willpower. You can't hide, and you can't blame anyone. That's why winning alone feels so pure—and losing alone teaches you lessons you can't learn any other way.

Doubles is a different kind of honesty. It's about communication, trust, and learning to take up space when your partner needs you and step back when it's their turn to lead. The court becomes wider, the points faster, and the strategy almost chess-like.

Both formats shaped me. Both taught me discipline and humility. And both made the rules of tennis feel less like rules and more like a rhythm my body learned before my mind caught up.

Tennis may look complex from the outside, but once you understand the heartbeat of it—serve, rally, point, game, set, match—you appreciate its beautiful simplicity. Like anything in life, the real meaning isn't in the scoring or the boundaries; it's in how you show up between the lines. Explaining tennis feels a lot like explaining the journey behind it. The rules are just the framework; the real story is what you do with them.

A player could have demolished the competition and then gone up against another player in the next round who just squeaked by, and that other player could still beat them by winning two out of three sets. Anyone can win at any time. It's so hard to predict because anyone can have an off day, when they are not playing well, especially with the sport being so mentally taxing.

Junior players have to keep track of their own scores. I struggled to track my score during games. My father bought me a score tracker for the court. That helped me keep track of where I was in the game and know if another player had miscounted their score or was cheating.

TENNIS COURTS

Tennis is played on four main surfaces. Hard courts are usually blue or green, and they're composed of a synthetic or acrylic surface laid over a concrete or asphalt foundation, which is very hard (surprise!). Clay courts are made of clay (another surprise, right?) and you can slide on them. However, clay courts are "slower," meaning you can't move around them as quickly as you can on a hard court. Super-athletic players who move quickly do well on clay courts, which are red or green. Real clay courts are common in Europe and in South America. In the US, what's called a clay court is artificial clay made up of crushed metabasalt, a type of volcanic rock, not brick like red clay courts. This crushed stone is a natural green material, most famously marketed as Har-Tru, and is installed over a porous base of crushed stone aggregate to create a durable and stable playing surface. The third type of court is grass, like you see at Wimbledon. The grass is cut so low to the ground that you can bounce a ball on it, sort of like the grass you see on a golf course. Grass courts are extremely fast. You'll find them in England and Germany, but rarely in the United States. They're difficult to maintain, which is why most countries moved to hard, clay, and other surfaces such as rubber, and carpet with sand on it. Rubber courts are rare. They're spongy. Carpet and sand courts are also rare. They're fast, and you can slide on them.

THE GRAND SLAM

The Grand Slam is the Super Bowl of tennis. Four Grand Slams are played annually.

In January, the Australian Open is played on a blue acrylic hard court at Melbourne Park in Melbourne. The French Open occurs in May-June. It's played on a clay court at Stade Roland-Garros in Paris. Wimbledon happens in June-July and is played on a grass court at the All England Lawn Tennis and Croquet Club in Wimbledon, Merton, an outer borough of London located eight miles from the city proper. The US Open is played in August-September on a hard court at the biggest stadium in the world, the USTA Billie Jean King National Tennis Center, in Queens, New York. Each Grand Slam carries equal weight in the tennis world, but Wimbledon has the most heritage and prestige of the four.

THE PENDLETON SCHOOL

The Pendleton School was on the IMG campus. I had the usual core courses—math, English, science, and history—plus one elective, either an art class or a language class. Anything more cut into tennis time, so Pendleton focused on the minimum requirements for graduation. Classes lasted just two to two and a half hours a day, in forty-five-minute blocks. The lessons and homework were easy compared to what I had come from, like they were giving us just enough to get by. I didn't fault the teachers for this. They were probably encouraged to go easy on us and accommodate our heavy sports schedules. They expected us to miss school days and even weeks for tournaments.

Academically, IMG's Pendleton School was good enough to be accredited. The intense focus on sports left little time for anything else. I knew my education would suffer. They seemed to be about two years behind, with seventh graders being taught lessons I was familiar with from fifth grade. Back in Rochester, my parents had been strict about me doing my homework before anything else. I'd finish my homework on the bus ride home. They'd check it, and then I could play.

Pendleton didn't use textbooks. Each student brought a laptop to class, and the books, lessons, and homework were all online. Which meant students were online during class and not always paying attention to the lessons. The distractions were a source of frustration for teachers, who tried their best to keep students focused. I remember certain teachers who were impactful, like Mr. Pottegier, my English teacher. He was the first teacher to really get me interested in poetry and writing. Then there was Mr. Van, my middle school science teacher. We could bring up something about *The Lord of the Rings*—or anything else that interested him—and the whole lesson would switch to that. I loved the tangents he would go on. It would help the class go by faster. I also really liked my art teacher, Caui L. I'm no artist, but in his class I was able to paint these incredible pictures and sketch some pretty prominent photos. I still remember sketching Obama, and it actually looking like him. It was some crazy foreshadowing because he would talk about the art fair Art Basel in Miami and how he would go to it to see all the top artists' work. Who would have known this would be an event I'd frequent annually in Miami? I've grown to love "Basel time" in Miami.

THE CAFETERIA

Kitchen ladies served food in the cafeteria. We had little say as far as menu choices were concerned. Usually, there were three options, and you picked one. There were no special considerations for allergies or diet restrictions I recall, unlike today, where a lot of eating establishments offer vegan, vegetarian, and gluten-free choices. The food was good, though. If you didn't like it, you could buy pizza and sandwiches at the nearby cafe. Payments were made by an ID card every student wore everywhere all the time. Parents would put money into an account for their student, and charges made on the ID were paid from those accounts. Some students complained about the food constantly and ate every meal at the cafe. Not me, though. Eating in the cafeteria, I got to know the kitchen ladies, who were always nice to me. I enjoyed the food. It was healthy—no soda or junk food. I didn't realize until later in life that kids grew up eating unhealthy snacks and drinking Coke because I was never exposed to those things. We had Gatorade. In fact, the Gatorade Institute tried out new formulas on IMG students to test the products' impacts on performance.

Everything at the Academy was geared toward physical health and wellness. That included what students put into their bodies and what they kept out. The drug testing Gary Cohen warned us about during orientation was no joke. Half a dozen times a year, there would be a knock on your door and a voice saying, "Drug testing! Be in the mental conditioning building in ten minutes." The first time, I didn't realize it was a pee test, so naturally, being awakened in the middle of the night, the first thing I did was head to the bathroom. Big mistake. I ended up at the testing site for hours, drinking water and trying to go again. They wouldn't let me leave until I did. For this type of drug test, they would be in the bathroom with you. Not in the actual stall, but they would watch you enter the bathroom and ensure you had nothing in your hands or in your pants. Cheating on these drug tests was almost an immediate expulsion.

I never felt the need to have someone "pee for me," which is where you get someone who didn't smoke marijuana to pee in a balloon for you. Most of the people who resorted to these tactics had this pee taped to the inside of their groin to evade detection. They went through all that work just to be able to smoke weed in very precarious locations, since the whole campus was drug free. To me none of that was ever worth it, and I never took part. A goodie-two-shoes, maybe, but I cared too much about my future.

Students who did drugs could also drink a lot of water and pee ahead of the test, hoping to flush the evidence from their systems. I know that the school always caught somebody. A student would end up in Gary's office, making that horrible call to their parents.

The cafeteria was one of the few places on campus where boy and girl students of every age and sport gathered under one roof. I prided myself on being open to meeting everyone, so I always had someone to sit with. If I didn't recognize anyone, I'd walk up to an empty seat and ask the people at the table if I could join them. Then I'd engage with them, usually by talking about their training, practices, and games. I don't know where I learned to connect with people so quickly. Maybe by going to dinners with my parents and their friends. The skill definitely stuck, and to this day, I can usually engage with new people right away, with no uneasiness or awkward silences. It's not a forced skill, though because the more I practiced it, the more I became naturally interested in people. I wanted to know their backgrounds and all about their countries and cultures. IMG, with its global student body, supplied plenty of opportunities.

I met Moniquee in the cafeteria. She was six feet six, a confident basketball player from California. A few years my senior, Moniquee took me under her wing and introduced me to Black culture. We watched *106 & Park* on BET, which showed new music videos, from hip-hop to rap and reggae to R&B. The dorm living rooms had TVs, so she and I and a few other girls would gather there before lunch to see what was new.

In the early 2000s, CDs were the medium of choice for music. I had a boombox in my dorm room, and I carried a portable CD player and wore headphones around campus for a while before getting an iPod. Having an iPod was a big deal. I shared music with my friends, including Moniquee, who became one of my closest friends at IMG.

Everywhere she went, Moniquee stood out. Only one girl was taller—a seven-feet-one white girl named Mimi, also from California. The two knew each other, but they couldn't have been more different. Mimi was sort of shy and awkward; Moniquee stood straight and tall, proud of her height and afraid of nothing. They were friends, and they were my friends too.

Moniquee introduced me to other basketball players, both boys and girls. The boys basketball team was predominantly Black. Many soccer players were Black, too, and guys from both teams hung out together. I got a sort of crash course in Black culture through them, especially Black pop culture—how they spoke, what they talked about, and who they listened to.

Moniquee and the U17 men's national soccer team went to a different school than me, a small private school called Edison Academy. They would have to take a bus or shuttle there, since it wasn't on the IMG campus. I remember watching the soccer players head toward the bus and thinking, *Wow, they are so cool.* Each of them had their own swagger and charm. There was one who seemed to command the most attention, Freddy Adu. He was the first child prodigy outside of tennis that I ever knew about. Freddy was younger than the rest of the team, and it seemed like he was getting special attention. This wasn't by accident. He was considered to be the best in the world. He was always friendly with me. I tended to treat everyone the same regardless of how popular or famous they were. The academy numbs you like that. You become used to seeing professional athletes. Nothing fazes you.

Jozy Altidore was another player who I remember well. He was really talented and skilled. Moniquee introduced me to Andrew G., who I think was from New Jersey or New York, and Peri M. I felt special meeting all these soccer players. At the time they were two or more years older than me. Moniquee was probably three years older than them. She was a senior in high school, while I was probably in eighth or ninth grade. I'm so thankful for those days back with her and Erica, another basketball player. They taught me how to dance, which music was hot, and how to dress. I still remember lessons Moniquee taught me because back then I was really trying to get boys' attention with my clothing. It was too much at times. And she would say, "Dani, if you have your legs exposed, you shouldn't have your stomach exposed too. Pick one." I didn't always listen to her, but I always remembered what she said. I still follow a lot of her advice today when I'm getting dressed and want to look sexy but classy.

Up until that point, I had been raised like a typical white girl, even though my parents were Black and Puerto Rican. There were no other Puerto Rican girls at the Academy but plenty of Spanish-speaking Latinos from Mexico and South American countries like Venezuela and Colombia. I tried to fit in with the Spanish-speaking kids and started teaching myself Spanish when I was twelve. I'd find Spanish song lyrics online and read the translations so I'd understand the meaning. Then I'd practice singing them to memorize the words. From there, I put phrases and sentences together. My roommates helped me practice, too, and there was always at least one girl who spoke the language fluently. Since we communicated through Messenger, I practiced reading and writing Spanish.

Common languages crossed sports boundaries and connected people. Cuban golfers sat with Venezuelan soccer players in the cafeteria. It was an opportunity for them to speak their native language at a school where they were expected to speak English all day. They probably shared some culture that I didn't understand too.

I heard a lot of Spanish in the cafeteria and around campus, but students from other countries spoke other languages too: Russian, German, French, and a lot of Chinese and Japanese. For a lot of Black kids coming in from Southern states, especially those who hadn't traveled overseas, I believe the experience was quite a culture shock, but a good one because they could take what they learned home with them—a new understanding of the diversity of language, culture, and people.

MY PARENTS AND IMG

My parents came to every practice. They didn't stick around for my physical and mental conditioning sessions, but whenever I was on the court, they were there.

My dad was always plugged into his work, though, even during my practices, with an earpiece in one ear and his other ear tuned to me and tennis.

I lived at IMG Monday through Friday. My parents were there for every practice, every day. On Fridays, they picked me up, and I spent the weekend at home preparing for or taking part in a tournament. On Sunday evening, my parents would drop me off at IMG.

I didn't enjoy leaving the campus every weekend. Monday through Friday, students stuck to a rigorous schedule, but weekends at IMG were when we could let loose and go to the mall, or the movies, or other places like Busch Gardens. Weekends were for socializing. So I missed all of that, especially the mall experience that so many other kids had back then. There was no Amazon shopping, so the mall was where everyone hung out. I'd hear them talk about their weekends and wish I had been there too. In hindsight, I think my parents were so protective partly because that's their nature but also because they worried about me, as a young girl, around so many other kids they didn't know. They knew the campus was a safe environment, but anything could happen off campus. They were always looking out for me.

Not everyone followed the rules. Especially the no smoking and no alcohol rules. Kids got expelled for drinking, smoking weed, and sneaking off campus. One girl got pregnant. I heard of students who put Listerine bottles in the freezer to get the alcohol to rise to the top. I couldn't understand their thinking. Getting caught with contraband got you expelled. For a sip of mouthwash alcohol? I just didn't get it. However, I came from a strict household, and IMG felt like freedom to me. Students who came from lenient homes probably felt like the school, with all its rules, was a prison.

I never saw drugs at IMG. My parents and a teacher did a good job scaring me away from ever trying anything like that, and I never did. Even the thought of being around people who broke the rules terrified me. If someone talked about drinking or drugs, I left the conversation. The "in the presence of" rule wasn't lost on me, and risking my IMG life, and potentially my tennis career, wasn't worth those friendships.

It was heartbreaking seeing kids break the rules and throw away their futures. One very talented Black tennis player who was there on a scholarship got kicked out for drugs, and he never achieved his potential. We all thought he'd go pro, but it never happened.

My dad reminded me of that and how one decision can have the gravest consequences. For aspiring athletes, the risks are even higher. So few of them make it to the pros, and when they throw away that opportunity, they aren't just getting in a little trouble. Often, they are changing the trajectory of the rest of their lives and the lives of their families. Remember, some of the students' families were there with them at IMG. They had quit their jobs to be there and support their kids. The students had agents. All that went away when they broke a rule. They'd be sent home with no scholarship, no schooling, no training, and no means of financial support.

5

THE COME UP

By 2002, I was playing well enough for my parents to look at coaches to take me to the next level. They hired Nick Bollettieri. Nick coached the pros on campus. I couldn't believe he'd be giving me private tennis lessons.

Nick was the most expensive coach on campus, but my parents must have believed I was worth the investment. He was also the most famous tennis coach in the world. He coached more number-one players than anyone else. More Grand Slam champions. There was no one in the world I wanted to impress more than Nick Bollettieri.

Nick was already an older man when he coached me, probably in his early seventies. He always brought a hitting coach to hit balls to me, and he'd be on my side of the court, beside or behind me, arms crossed. He wore yellow-framed Oakley sunglasses, so I couldn't see his eyes, but I knew he watched my every move. Sometimes he wore a shirt, but most times, he was shirtless. He worked out at the gym every morning and was in excellent shape. Nick was always tan too. Between lessons, he'd lie outside with a metal sun reflector. He was the first person I saw do this in Florida since most people would just get tan naturally from the sun. He would put sun oil on and lie down with metal reflectors in between lessons. I'm not sure why he wanted to be so tan. His olive skin darkened the most from when he did the tanning.

People always liked to talk about Nick having eight wives in his lifetime. I was only ever close with his last one Cindi. He had grown children from some of his other wives, as I remember vividly some of his older children were already midway through life. His youngest daughter, Alex Bollettieri, was a grade or two older than me. I remember seeing her with her dad and thinking, *Wow, I wonder what it's like to have such a famous dad.* Danielle (Dani) Bollettieri, from what I can remember, was married to Greg Bruenick, whose title was senior vice president at IMG and director of IMG Academies. I would watch them golf cart around the campus, and I knew they were super connected to every major decision that was happening with the Academy. I loved how fit and happy she was, she would always smile and say hello to me on campus.

The wife that I connected with the most was his latest wife and widower, Cindi Bollettieri. I always admired her personality and the way she was such a supportive spouse to Nick. He was very loud and boisterous, and she complemented him so well with her beauty, intelligence, and wonderful smile. What was most notable was when they decided to adopt two young Black children. When I was younger, I always thought, *I wonder why they decided to do this, since they could really adopt anybody, since they appear to be Italian and European.* I don't know the backstory, but what I do know is they loved their two kids, Giovanni and Giacomo Bollettieri. I always loved how they had such Italian names. He was survived by seven and was inducted into the Tennis Hall of Fame not long before passing away at ninety-one, surrounded by loved ones.[2]

The first time I had a lesson with him, I was shaking. It was like meeting a celebrity and a hero. Nick stood behind me, arms crossed, watching me hit. I was incredibly nervous and not playing well. Once I settled into the lesson and hit better, he called my dad over.

"Look at this," he said. "Look at her arm. See what she's doing with her elbow? We've gotta pull her elbow in here. Then we have to do this..."

He continued his critique, and I tried to adjust myself on the fly. After all, this was a tennis god, and if I had any hope of amounting to anything, I had to follow his advice. After the lesson, Nick always praised me for what I did well and then told me what I needed to work on. The lessons were video recorded.

Working with Nick as my coach was incredible. He made me feel like the best tennis player in the world, building up my self-esteem. He brought out the best in me and made me feel important. I played some of my best tennis on his court. That experience showed me how important the mental game was. To play at the highest level, I had to believe in myself and my ability to play well. I still believe his secret for turning out so many professional players was less about physical skill and more about the confidence he instilled in people, convincing them they could win any match.

He didn't overlook poor playing and mistakes, though, and he'd tear you down for them. But the ratio was around eighty percent praise and twenty percent criticism. People have told me he wasn't always that way and that in the early days of his coaching career, he was a lot tougher. His students from the 1980s have mixed feelings about his approach, but my experience working with Nick was excellent.

I wondered if his shift in demeanor was a side effect of getting older and wiser and mellowing out, or if it was financially motivated. Parents paid hundreds of dollars, even $1,000 an hour, for Nick to coach their kids. Nick was a coach but also a savvy businessperson. Remember, he started the Academy. He may have figured he'd keep more clients by giving them a pleasant experience instead of a traumatic one. Think about it. He began to realize how much of an idol he was to these kids and especially the tennis parents, and he boosted the kids' self-esteem, letting them know how good they were or saying that he saw "greatness within them." I can equate this to when Tony Robbins or any self-help guru gives a workshop or a speech. Do they believe what they are saying? Yes, absolutely. But are they also getting paid an awful lot of money to make people feel a certain way despite what they really feel inside? Yes, they are. So because of that, I learned as I got older that his impact was more about how he made you feel versus teaching you the *X*'s and *O*'s of tennis.

I was late for six o'clock practice only twice in my tennis career. The first time was for a morning group practice while in Coach Jairo's group. I woke up to my alarm clock, hit the snooze button, and promptly fell back to sleep. To my surprise, once I rolled over and rechecked my phone, I found that I had slept another thirty minutes, which now made me ten minutes late. When I showed up late for practice, the coaches made everyone run "suicides," sprinting from one end of the court to the next and back ten times. I was so ashamed of having put the other players through that. I wanted to disappear. What was worse than the feeling of being late and trying to frantically get ready for the practice knowing damn well that I was going to be in trouble was the way that instead of making me run, I was forced to watch the other kids run. These weren't just kids in my group. This was the entire boys and girls tennis program. This was extremely embarrassing, and it changed everything inside me when it came to being early, on time, or late. Experiencing the embarrassment and shame of causing other people to be punished because of me left me never wanting to feel that way ever again.

The next time I was late was for a private lesson with Nick.

Training with him had become the highlight of my day. So when I slept through my alarm the morning of a lesson, my heart dropped. I was supposed to be on the court at six thirty, and it was six forty-five!

I rushed to get dressed and hurried to the court. My parents were already there. I had five missed calls from my dad. *Yikes*, I thought. *This isn't going to be good.*

I worried about Nick being mad, but he was nothing compared to my mom and dad. The looks on their faces! A mix of anger, embarrassment, and disappointment. My punishment was doing suicides.

At least this time, no one else had to run them, but it was still awful. After that, I got a second alarm, a backup. I was never late again to anything sports related for the rest of my career.

I trained under Nick for several years. And I was never late for a lesson again.

MENTAL, MEDIA, AND PERSONALITY TRAINING

Nick worked on my physical training and tennis exclusively. For mental conditioning, in addition to the group training provided by IMG, my personal coach was Trevor Moawad. I had only a few sessions with Trevor, and he went on to bigger things, including coaching NFL athletes. At the time, I didn't appreciate how useful mental training was, but as I competed at higher levels, I understood the importance of the mental game in tennis. Trevor's instruction helped a lot.

Tennis players are socially awkward. Think about it: they play at a very young age, commit most of their time to tennis, and neglect social skill development. They don't often communicate with people who don't play sports.

I was unique in that respect. My parents took me everywhere with them, and I was used to sitting at the grownups' table and holding conversations. Strangers didn't make me nervous. Still, I enjoyed media training at IMG.

Steve Shenbaum, a former actor known for creating the consultancy Game On Nation, partnered with IMG to provide this training. Steve stepped us through games and scenarios that helped us prepare for interviews, especially those that happened right after a match, when an athlete can be caught off guard and unprepared to talk about the outcome. We practiced mock interviews. Steve brought in Blair Bloomston to be his partner at Game On, and it was an honor to watch the incredible work they did with so many athletes.

The after-match interviews were never difficult for me, in part because my dad recorded all my matches and we reviewed them together. I was used to answering questions about my performance. I was also used to keeping my emotions in check when discussing my losses. My dad had trained me to critique myself objectively and without getting angry or upset.

Steve also worked with us on personality training. He taught us how to be less stoic and more engaging—priceless work for the shyest players, and there were many. We learned how to put more of ourselves into interviews, so the conversation wasn't only about the sport. One exercise I remember well was coin practice. We had to come up with five or six "coins," with each one representing something about us that most people didn't know and made us unique. That way, if we were asked a question and didn't know how to answer, we'd go to a coin and talk about it instead.

I liked the training but probably got less out of it than other students. I was a natural extrovert who made friends quickly. When I met someone for the first time, I tried to find something we had in common right away. I might ask where they're from, for instance. Since I'd traveled a lot, the odds of my visiting their country, state, or city were high! I tried to get them talking about themselves while I listened.

TOURNAMENTS

I played in tournaments almost every weekend. If my dad couldn't find a match for me, I would play in the Academy's Grand Prix. All the groups took part in the Grand Prix, so I could be up against a girl in my group or from another group, including Coach Percy's. Each student got a report card every week showing the results of their matches.

After my first couple of years at IMG, I was flying around the country on weekends to play in USTA tournaments. Eventually, I flew around the world, playing in junior ITF tournaments.

Nick had instilled in me a confidence I never knew I had. My playing improved. Everything clicked. When I went up against players who always beat me, the matches were closer. I started beating players I'd never won against before.

On April twenty-three, 2004, I competed in the Academy's monthly Grand Prix. The Grand Prix tournament had a huge draw, with thirty-six to forty-eight players. After each round, the winners played against each other, and the losers were eliminated. This continued until there were two players remaining, who then played the finals.

I played three matches, first against an older girl in my level, Mary Chupa. I won that match. Then I beat two girls from higher groups, including Akbota, a girl from Kazakhstan who I lost against the prior two times we played.

My next opponent was Jessica C., a star player from France. She was in Percy's group. I was still in the second group. I never won against Coach Percy's girls in practice; heck, they would rarely have people in Coach Jairo's group compete against Percy's group because it wouldn't be worth it for Percy's girls. The coaches never pitted me against them in practice, probably to spare me from complete and utter humiliation. So why now?

My defeat was a foregone conclusion, and sure enough, Jessica came in strong from the get-go, winning the first set six–1.

With nothing to lose (but my dignity), I called on all the positivity I could muster and went all out, more aggressive than ever before. All those hours of training with Nick, where he made me believe that as long as I did my best, good things could happen, pushed me to go hard.

Then, something changed. I started coming back, and Jessica got flustered.

In tennis, it's all about gaining the momentum and maintaining it until the bitter end. Keep your foot on the gas the whole time, or your opponent snatches it back. Once you lose that momentum, it's tough to regain it. When I came on strong and started winning, the energy shifted. Suddenly, I was driving the game.

In the second set, I beat Jessica seven–6. It was a narrow win, but enough to send my confidence soaring. Jessica threw her racket and swore—in French, but I knew enough to understand the sentiment. She was so much better than I on paper, yet here I was, on track to win. That must have gotten to her, and she spiraled from there. Negativity kills you on the court.

Then I won the third set. Visibly shaken, Jessica offered her limp hand at the net. I shook it.

We both knew this was a huge turning point. No one expected me to win. It was one thing to have beaten a player in one set because practice sets happened all the time at IMG. To win an entire match that had something on the line was huge for me. I could see the other coaches were shocked.

Beating Jessica in the semifinals put me into the tournament finals.

I played against Carling Seguso. She was one of my best friends at IMG, the daughter of Carling Bassett-Seguso and Robert Seguso. They were a professional tennis family, with both parents playing at the highest levels. Robert won Grand Slams in doubles and was number one in the world, and Carling Bassett reached a career singles high of number eight in the world.

Carling trained at IMG back in the 1980s and was one of the first major pros to come out of Nick's group. Playing Carling Jr in the finals was tough. It's always hard to play against your friends, especially when everybody is watching and someone has to win and lose. Tennis is so emotional. I knew I needed to give my all to this match to finally get the respect I thought I deserved on campus. People already viewed Carling in a positive way; she was playing really well and hitting the crap out of the ball. She always had the most beautiful forehand technique. I attribute it to the coaching from her dad, and also the Wilson racket she used. The ball would leave her racket, and it would sound so beautiful and clean off of her strings. Somehow, I won the first set, and I kept winning. I won the tournament.

My parents were glowing, especially my dad. To him, winning was everything. It was as if, for a brief moment, all the pressure and intensity lifted. I felt like I was on cloud nine, and I couldn't be higher in the air. More important than school, and even more important than being a good kid. When Dad was happy, my world was a better place. I had another trophy to put on the growing trophy wall, and it was a big one. The feeling was short-lived. Next week there would be another tournament and another chance to prove myself against someone else. I was only as good as I was yesterday, so I had to make every day count.

No one at IMG took players seriously until they won tournaments. Before this tournament, I was an afterthought, someone to laugh at or make fun of. Now people saw me differently. They took me seriously. Coaches who'd never given me the time of day praised me, said they "always believed in me."

They pulled my dad aside, telling him how good I was and what I could become. They weren't on the court with me all those hours and days with Jimmy Nagelsen and Nick Bollettieri, but suddenly, they were everywhere. Finally, I was accepted. I was a real tennis player.

That year taught me a lot about winning. I finally understood that everyone's journey is their own. Instead of comparing myself to other people, I had to focus on myself and do my best. Putting in the hours, the practice, the diligence, did something all the comparisons and worry could never do. It made me a better player. It made me a winner, not only in my eyes but in the eyes of all the doubters, the non-believers. The people who saw me as an afterthought.

I wasn't just a rich "spoiled" kid whose parents paid for a bunch of lessons, hoping their little tennis player would someday make it. I had the guts and the drive to do what it took to win. And now I was proving it where it counted—on the court.

In particular, the tennis academy director, Gabe Jaramillo, believed in me. Gabe walked around the campus like he owned the place, and for good reason. Everyone respected him. Only Coach Nick was held in higher regard. Gabe wore his signature flat-brimmed brown hat, which gave him this unique prominent appeal. Two covered parking spaces by the dorms were reserved for Gabe's white Porsche Boxster and his 911. He liked to bring his massive dog onto the campus grounds. It was the biggest dog I had ever seen.

After the tournament, IMG moved me into Coach Percy's group. Later, I learned that Gabe was one of the main reasons I moved into Percy's group. IMG rarely made transfers midyear, but because of my results, and because people like Gabe believed in me, I finally earned my spot and my respect. He built so many champions. Nick is the face and gets so much of the credit, but Gabe was the rock and the one we all wanted to impress.

6

FROM DREAM TO REALITY

Going from "Danielle the afterthought" to "Danielle—she can play" came with more pressure. I was playing alongside star players.

At nine years old, Michelle Larcher de Brito was the youngest in the group. She started at IMG after me, and her parents moved to Bradenton from Portugal to be with their daughter. They brought her older twin brothers too. Imagine relocating your entire family for a dream of being a professional tennis player. Everything was riding on that decision. Michelle was the number-one player in Portugal for her age, dominating the Junior European circuit. She was playing in ITF tournaments and winning them at an extremely young age. She always had phenom energy and got a lot of attention because she was *it*. Throughout her entire junior career (until the very end), Michelle never lost a match. I couldn't relate to this at all. I lost *all the time*. So I had plenty of practice walking up to the net to shake the hand of an opponent who'd just beat me. I won, too, but I lost more tournaments than some of the other girls in Coach Percy's group.

Other star players in Percy's group—now, my group—included

Tamaryn "Tammy" Hendler from South Africa (who later played for Belgium) and Tara Moore from England. Michelle, Tammy, and Tara were all signed with IMG agents. Jessica C. from France, Heather Watson and Jordane Dobbins from England, and Nicole Bartnik (Nicki) and Mary Clayton from the US were in the group too. Nicki and I became good friends. Later, Percy's group added Vicky Duval and Sachia Vickery, two other young up-and-coming junior players who were beginning to create a buzz. Mallory Cecil was also added a little later too. She ended up winning the NCAA national championship for Duke as a freshman and had a professional career after reaching a career high of number 365 in the world. Mary played with Mallory at Duke and was a member of the national championship team. She was the youngest sister of a tennis powerhouse family. Nicole ended up becoming a two-time Ivy League Player of the Year for Columbia and was inducted into the Athletics Hall of Fame. As a junior, she reached a career high of number eighty-six in the world. As I write this book, only Heather and Sachia are still playing on the WTA tour. Heather has reached a career high of number thirty-eight in the world, and Sachia has reached a career high of number seventy-three in the world. All the others had their careers and have moved on to other things. Michelle reached a career high of number seventy-six in the world. Tammy reached a career high of #178 in the world. Tara reached a career high of #146 in singles and seventy-seven in doubles. Vicky reached a career high of number eighty-seven in the world. I was in very good company in this group; being surrounded by so many incredible players only caused my level to rise.

Coach Percy was from Peru. He was an amazing coach, like Nick, but that was where the similarities ended. Percy wore an enormous straw hat and spoke with a strong Peruvian accent. He put zinc sunscreen under his eyes. No sunbathing for Percy. He avoided the sun like it was the plague, always trying to cover his arms and face.

The group's dynamic was different from Coach Jairo's. There was camaraderie but also competitiveness. Everyone wanted to be Percy's favorite player. Girls vied for his attention, and he leveraged that vibe to motivate them to compete harder. He praised the girls who were winning, but he also criticized them. Any attention, good or bad, made a girl feel as if Coach Percy cared about her. Being ignored was the worst.

At first, I was thrilled to be in a group of prestigious tennis players. *I've proven myself*, I thought. Yet being in the top group wasn't enough. I had to keep winning, week after week, or risk losing everyone's respect and approval. Being in Coach Jairo's group was nothing compared to this. Sure, I wanted to win every game, but it never felt like a life-or-death situation. No one expected me to win every time in that group. Now I had to win every single time I played against a girl in a lower group. I felt as if my newfound esteem could be snatched away any day. All it took was losing to one girl in one match.

Suddenly, Jessica's anger at the Grand Prix made a lot more sense to me. Losing to me changed her status. Players and coaches poked at her. They felt comfortable putting more pressure on her. She was always giving me the side eye, like I was the cause of her problems. Which I was, sort of.

The other coaches treated me differently once I was in Percy's group. They were friendlier and more open. They acknowledged me, and I no longer felt invisible. The coaches were interested in my life and genuinely seemed to care about my tennis career, even approaching me on campus to ask about upcoming tournaments.

The other players treated me differently too, especially girls in lower tennis groups. Most of them were very supportive of my sudden promotion. A handful of girls in the group just below Percy's group resented me, though. I had leapfrogged past them to snag a coveted spot in the top group, a spot they felt they deserved. Part of their anger arose from the fact that group changes usually only happened once a year. You were given your group at the beginning of the year, and you stayed there for the entire year. I was moved midyear, catching everyone by surprise. In an environment ruled by organization and schedules, the sudden switch made people uneasy.

Playing for Percy, the mentality was different. In Coach Jairo's group, the kids were happy to be in a group playing tennis at IMG. They didn't seem very concerned about winning. In Coach Percy's group, the girls were hyper-focused on the next match, the next tournament, whether it was at IMG or somewhere else around the world.

Every girl was training for something in England, Brazil, Australia, France, Mexico, or Serbia. Everyone was on a mission to win. In Coach Jairo's group, I was the only girl whose parents showed up for practices. In Percy's group, other parents were present. Michelle's parents. Tammy's parents. Tara's mom. My parents sat with them in the bleachers. By then, I was used to my parents dissecting every practice. There were more younger girls playing by then, too—girls who had come with their parents from other countries. These girls weren't focused on being good at IMG—they were set on changing their futures and the futures of their families. They all planned to go pro. There was no plan B.

For some girls, tennis was their financial future. Being agented by IMG came with perks. Students didn't pay for training, housing, or meals. They essentially had a free ride, and their parents were housed in apartments across the street from the campus. Those perks came with pressure. I caught glimpses of it occasionally—stress on the girls' faces, knowing their families' futures depended on them. It was a lot for a kid.

Staying on Percy's good side became my mission. I didn't think I had the talent some of the other girls had, but I had my work ethic, instilled in me at a young age. Also, I wasn't shy about campaigning for myself. I got in front of Coach Percy whenever I could. Did the extra work. Showed him what I could do.

There were seven of us in the group initially. Practicing with them showed me I could beat two of them regularly. I never beat some of them, like Michelle or Tammy, but I came close in some tight three-set matches, and even a Grand Prix final where I lost to Tammy. My goal—in addition to gaining Percy's approval—was to beat almost half of them on any given day.

I hit one goal early on. We were doing forehand drills. A backhand shot takes two hands. A forehand shot takes one hand. It's usually the biggest shot—the kind that wins games.

Players lined up on one side of the net. Coach Percy stood on the opposite side with a shopping cart full of tennis balls. He hit a ball over the net, and we took turns hitting it back with a forehand. There was usually footwork involved to get to the ball, and we were supposed to hit it as hard as possible while keeping it on the court instead of hitting the fence on the other side. The best shots took power, athleticism, and skill. If a girl hit the fence, Percy got mad.

My turn came, and I hit the ball as hard as I could. It was a clean forehand, and Percy complimented me. "Nice one, Danielita!" he said. He called me Danielita in that accent, and I never corrected him. I liked when he called me that because it showed me that he knew and acknowledged my Puerto Rican history. I can still hear him now yelling, "Tenga!"—which kind of means "take that" in English—as we completed the forehand drill, with each girl hitting it harder and flatter than the last. I could hear the crack of the ball as it left each girl's racket.

Tennis is a mental game in many ways. I'd learned that from Coach Nick. The sport also requires physical fitness and endurance. Sometimes, winning comes down to outlasting the opponent. It wasn't enough to be talented. We had to hit hard and make every shot longer than the competition's.

Coach Percy focused on physicality. He encouraged us to be aggressive without sacrificing skill or stamina. We had to stay on the court for thirty, forty, even fifty shots per point. It was exhausting. I had to pace myself.

Tennis isn't like other sports. Except maybe boxing. Imagine punching somebody as hard as you can. Now imagine doing that for two minutes, and for twelve rounds. You couldn't keep it up, so you'd have to be strategic about when you punched and when you defended yourself.

Tennis has different styles. Aggressive players go for every shot.

They don't last long on the court, so they try to end the point quickly. It's a risky strategy that can pay off with big rewards as long as they keep hitting winning shots. If they don't, or if the other player keeps hitting the ball back, they can wear out.

Counterpunchers mimic the opponent's pace, not going for winning shots but just hitting the ball back every time. They use less energy while they wait for the other player to wear out and miss. Serve-and-volley players hit the serve and come up to the net to make contact with the ball as a volley, not letting the ball touch the ground and bounce before they make contact.

Later tennis players would focus on fitness. They learned to win by lasting on the court versus hitting one winning shot—"winner"—after another. The game developed as we learned more about physical training and recovery.

My longest match lasted six or seven hours. I didn't take a bathroom break, and I only snacked on bananas and Cliff bars. Technically, you can take a bathroom break between sets. I didn't always take one because I didn't want to lose my momentum. Matches could go on late into the night. I played an ITF match in Tulsa, Oklahoma, that went on until three in the morning due to rain delays.

A player could play for hours one day, then have to come back and play again the next day. Recovery became increasingly important. A rested player has a tremendous advantage over one who's sore, tired, and potentially cramping.

I dialed in my cool-down and recovery routine, jogging, stretching, and icing my muscles after every match. If Normatec compression boots were available, I used them too. I stayed out of the sun, ate, and slept. Even when my adrenaline was high, I was always exhausted enough to sleep.

THE EDDIE HERR TOURNAMENT

The Eddie Herr Tournament is one of the most important junior tournaments in the world, attracting the best players to compete.

Held annually at the Academy, it was my chance to see how players in other countries operated compared to students at IMG. Players from Russia and Eastern European countries like the Czech Republic came with their coaches and parents. Each year there are more than fifty countries represented in that tournament, a true melting pot from around the world. I heard lots of disturbing stories—and saw some of them play out—during large junior tournaments where people from around the world came together to play.

I soon learned firsthand that tennis parents can be the worst sports parents in the world, and tennis coaches can be cruel. The abuse wasn't doled out in the open, but it was obvious. You might stumble upon it in a hallway or outside, behind bushes and trees. If a child lost a match, they'd be beaten. A girl who performed poorly might have all her hair cut off.

As wonderful as tennis can be for a child, in the wrong hands, it can be miserable. Adults responsible for protecting children in their care used their authority to threaten and punish them. Most of these stories will never be told, but some find their way into the spotlight. Like the story of the girl who found fame when she became the number-one player at a very young age. When she lost a junior tournament, her mother broke the girl's wrist, forcing her to play the whole tournament with her other hand. Somehow, she still won the tournament.

In tennis, and especially in the juniors, there are about five tournaments that really matter. The Junior Grand Slams are the highest level, and just below them is the Eddie Herr, which takes place at IMG. Then there are the Orange Bowl, which takes place in Miami; the Copa Casablanca, which takes place in Mexico; and the Copa Gerdau, which takes place in Brazil. There are probably a handful of others that have been added since I stopped playing juniors, but it's inevitable that something intense is going to go down in any of these events because the best players in the world are competing for the right to say they are *still* the best in the world.

No doubt, fear tactics are found in every sport. They seem to be more prevalent in young girls' sports like tennis and gymnastics. The stress leads to other problems, like eating disorders, which are one of the worst things that can happen to a tennis player. You cannot play well if you don't get enough of the right foods and calories, period.

My father knew that I, as an American with a supportive family of means, had trouble understanding certain concepts. Still, to compete, I needed to be as tough as girls who weren't so lucky. Before competing against players from certain countries, he'd remind me, "They will do anything to beat you, Danielle. If they could poke your eye out, they would. Their parents depend on them financially, and if they lose, the whole family may not eat for a week. Losing could mean a beating for the girl, or having her head shaved." I hated hearing this, but I understood why he did it. Back then, American girls were not dominating in tennis, and the stakes probably had something to do with that. Disappointing my parents was one thing. If losing meant a physical punishment or having my hair shaved off to prove a point, I'd definitely play harder. My parents had to create an environment that was more challenging than it really was so I could compete hard against these girls. Most of these Eastern European girls would be hard as nails, and nothing fazed them. I could only imagine some of the things they had to endure growing up in war-torn countries. There is something about experiencing and seeing extreme levels of adversity and discomfort that makes you a stronger player physically, but mostly mentally.

The pressure to win also led to cheating on the court. High-level tournaments have a chair umpire. In junior tennis, players rely on an honor system, calling their own lines—whether the ball falls inside or outside the lines. If the ball fell near a line, girls under the most pressure to win called it in their own favor, often lying to win the point. Players argued back and forth, which was probably a tactic in itself—wearing out the other player by making them angry and getting in their head.

In March 2008, I played in an ITF junior tournament in El Salvador. I was there with my coach at the time, Lance Luciani, and representatives from IMG. In the finals, after three rounds of wins, I played against Lauren McHale, the other seeded player in the draw, and won. I had never won a singles tournament at the ITF junior level, so this was a big deal. I had gotten to the finals a few times, and to the semifinals or quarterfinals, but I had not won the whole tournament in singles until this moment. I wished my parents had been there to see it, but this was one of the few tournaments they missed.

After that, I started having really good results in the junior circuit at a world level. My ranking jumped up, and finally I was one of the top one hundred girls *in the world* competing in the eighteen and under division. This meant I could now play the Junior Grand Slams.

The tournament victories and strong showings weren't just about tennis rankings or getting into the right training group. They represented something much deeper: the validation that all the sacrifices, all the intense focus, all the single-minded dedication was actually leading somewhere.

When you're living that life, where every aspect of your waking existence and every breath you take is geared toward becoming a champion, you need those concrete markers of progress. You need proof that the path you're on—the one that requires you to give up so much of what other teenagers take for granted—is actually the right one.

That's what people don't understand about pursuing elite-level athletics. They assume it's just, "Oh yeah, you put a lot of work in," but they don't know how every aspect of your life, every decision you make, is filtered through one question: "How does this help me become a champion?"

That whole energy behind it, that mindset—anything that's distracting you from that goal becomes a problem. There's a reason the people who are the best in the world at something are not good at other things. They can't focus on everything at once. They have to focus on the one thing they need to be the best in the world at.

That El Salvador tournament—whether it was the specific catalyst or just one of many steppingstones—represented that moment when the sacrifice started to pay off in measurable ways. When the dream stopped being just a dream and started becoming a reality you could point to on a results sheet.

TROUBLE ON CAMPUS

I avoid gossip, but sometimes it's impossible to ignore. In early January 2009, the whole campus was buzzing. "Did you hear what happened to Gabe?"

My parents were at IMG that day. When we finally got word, we couldn't believe it: Gabe Jaramillo and a couple of other guys, including vice presidents Ted Meekma and Greg Breunich and chief financial officer Jeff McNeil, had been asked to leave. Gabe was escorted off campus. The reasons they were dismissed were never fully discussed, but news articles alluded to financial disagreements.[3]

The news came as a shock to everyone. Here was a guy we truly idolized, and then he was gone—whisked away by men in uniform. His parking spots, suddenly empty, were a painful reminder that whatever was happening behind the scenes was finally going to come to light, and *everything* was going to change. The culture of the program seemed to change after that. A weight seemed to have lifted, and it wasn't until after he left that I realized how much the energy changed.

IMG Academy did not give second chances. Not to students who broke the rules. Not to coaches or administrators. I never saw Gabe step foot on the IMG campus again. So much time has passed. Who knows what he looks like today. I always wished him well and still remember the impact he had on me and my game.

IMG is still home to the Eddie Herr tournament for juniors and that still yields the best players in all age groups from the whole world. If he were to come back, it would be for that, but from what I understand, mostly he only travels with a player at this point if they are playing in a Grand Slam.

I didn't know what to think about the situation. In addition to the absolute shock of it all, the timing was awful for me. I had just joined Coach Percy's group and was getting on good terms with Gabe. He really seemed to believe in me, and I thought he could help my career. We had built a strong rapport. Now I had to start all over again, proving myself to his replacement, Chip Brooks, who I had known, but just like in any company, when regimes and structures change, everyone has to adjust. Turns out Chip and I ended up getting along well. His son, Jared Brooks, was a year older than me, but he was in some of my classes at the Pendleton School, so I had that connection point. It would take some adjusting but we all learned to love Chip and what he brought to that director role.

Later, I learned that Gabe opened up his own academy in South Florida with the blueprint he learned from Nick. It's pretty success-ful from what I've heard and is a training ground for a lot of active touring pros and aspiring pros.

GAINING CONFIDENCE

On a good day, I was beating half the people in Coach Percy's group. That had been my goal. The best players in the group were play-ing pro tournaments and sometimes winning them. That made me believe that going pro was within my reach.

Instead of dreaming about it, being a professional tennis player was now a foregone conclusion. Of course I'd turn pro. It was the only logical next step.

Prior to that time, I never believed I'd make it. Little Danielle back in Rochester played tennis and made her parents smile. Young Danielle watched it happen for other people, but never believed she belonged within their ranks. But teenage Danielle—this girl who beat Jessica and was beating half the girls on Percy's team—was a very different Danielle, and she was going pro. In a way, I felt like I was on a reality show. IMG presented me with challenge after challenge and made me a different person. It made me a serious tennis player and a formidable opponent. If we are speaking of reality shows, IMG was a mix of three prominent reality shows: *Amazing Race* because we were traveling all over the world and adding pages to our passport books, *Big Brother* because the IMG walls were high and there were cameras everywhere watching your every move and ensuring you wouldn't leave or anybody else would come in, and *Survivor* because you needed to play strategically. You had alliances and frenemies. You also needed to survive week over week and not get kicked out. Overall, the experience was a wild one.

My parents' demeanor never changed during this time. No matter how well I did, they didn't shower me with praise. Occasionally, I'd catch one of them doing a fist pump when I scored a point, but they never said they were proud of me back then. I thought that was weird because I saw the other kids' parents tell them how good they were. My mother and father didn't praise me until much later, after my tennis career. I could have used some kind words from them back then, but maybe they were afraid I'd get too relaxed and stop focusing on winning. We were always focusing on what was next. There wasn't much time allotted to basking in the blissful feeling of a win. There was another match always to prepare for, another tournament, another country, another airport, another hotel room.

Seeking validation mattered to me then, and it still matters. It's part of my personality. If I'm not seeking external approval from my parents, I'm looking to my boss, my peers, my clients. But mostly, my parents. Looking back on my training and early career, I played best when someone believed in me—Nick, Gabe, and other coaches. If they believed in me and they told me they believed in me, I believed in me too.

I was still attending classes at the Pendleton School and taking only the core classes required to graduate. With all the other demands on my schedule, there wasn't room for electives. I needed time for practice and tournaments. When the school switched up my schedule and I had to attend school in the morning, I'd get up extra early and play tennis before classes. No matter what, I always played tennis before and after school. In the evenings, I attended study hall at the school, where tutors helped students catch up on schoolwork and prepare for college. I missed a lot of classes, so I took advantage of study hall time.

Classes lasted about two hours a day, and as busy as I was with tennis, I loved school. This was an opportunity to interact with people outside the tennis program in a noncompetitive environment. It was also an opportunity to catch my breath. I was exhausted all the time from all of the training and practice I was doing. I was nonstop from the moment my feet hit the floor. I made friends with kids who played soccer, basketball, baseball, and football. Tennis felt like work. Aside from the cafeteria and after dinner, school was the only time to relax and socialize.

I got to talk to boys in class, and there were a lot of them. Since there were more boys sports than girls, the ratio of boys to girls was about five to one. Some of them acted up, as if they didn't care about getting in trouble. Not me. I was a by-the-rules kid. I earned A's in everything except math, but I scraped by with a C or a B– every year. No one cared about my grades, but I liked school and took a lot of pride in my academic achievement. I wanted to do well in everything, not just tennis. The attitude was "just do whatever it takes to graduate. Who cares if you are getting A's. Are you winning?" This was never said to me, but the energy I felt surrounding this was palpable.

Pendleton School uniforms included a polo shirt with the letter *P* on the front and khaki pants. I didn't think about it at the time, but the uniforms probably prevented the shaming and bullying that went on in public schools where the discrepancies between kids whose parents could afford nice clothes and those who couldn't were obvious. There were no nerd groups, popular kid groups, or jock groups. Cliques didn't exist. Everybody was an athlete.

I noticed a difference in how students interacted based on their sport, though. The attitudes of players in team sports like basketball were different from those of us playing individual sports, like tennis. Basketball players supported each other. If one was having a bad day, he could count on his teammates to hold him up. In girls' tennis, even though we played in groups under a coach, we weren't a team. We competed. We were cordial, but we didn't share the same camaraderie I saw among the soccer, baseball, and basketball players.

THE ALWAYS PRESENT "IN THE PRESENCE OF" RULE

I remembered the "in the presence of" rule for a long time. Since my parents picked me up every Friday to spend the weekend at home, I was seldom in an environment where a rule could be broken. I didn't go to the mall or to the movies with the other kids. All my socializing was done on campus, where getting into trouble was possible but not easy. If I did sense a situation was going in a direction I didn't like, I left.

There were ways around the rules if you were careful. Some girls dressed in baggy clothes and hoodies to sneak into the boys' dorms. Since the cameras were pointed at students' backs, getting into the dorms was easy. Leaving with a camera pointed at your face was harder.

A couple of girls on the golf team and boys on the soccer team hooked up on the tennis courts. I guess they didn't know about the cameras.

Getting away with anything was difficult. If you weren't being spied on by a camera, there was always the campus staff patrolling the area. Their key rings gave them away, though. You could hear them coming by the jingle-jangle of keys hanging off their belts. If you paid attention, you learned their schedules and knew when they patrolled the campus. I was a rule-follower, but I wasn't a goody-two-shoes. Maybe I didn't break rules, but I got very good at bending them. I was a teenage girl. As a tennis player, I knew where all the cameras were.

THE 100 PERCENT EFFORT AWARD

The IMG tennis program holds a banquet and awards ceremony at the end of every school year. After my second year, my parents and I were enjoying our banquet meals and listening to the speaker talk about someone who came to the Academy as a beginner player who showed little promise. This girl got up early every day and headed to the courts to practice shots before group training. She took extra lessons, worked hard, and, over time, showed incredible improvement. Whoever they were talking about sounded like a real superstar. When the speaker said my name, I was shocked. I'd never even heard of the one hundred Percent Effort Award, and there I was, winning it. That award meant so much to me. The decision to give it to me was subjective—not based on winning a match but on people noticing me and wanting to acknowledge my hard work.

I was so proud of that award, and I think my parents were proud of it, and me, too. The coaches congratulated me and told me I deserved it, that I had earned it. After all the work I put in to improve and change people's impressions of me, to get them to see me as a serious player, that felt good—like my determination and effort were finally paying off.

PLAYING PRO

In 2005, I played my first pro tournament. I don't remember all the details, except it was in Texas; and I lost.

The tournament was my first chance to play for pro points. A few weeks later, I played my second pro tournament. I remember that one much better.

My dad signed me up to play a $10,000 tournament in Morelia, Mexico. In the world of tennis, that's not a lot of money. It's the lowest level. Prize money at tournaments like Wimbledon and the US Open runs from $3 to $4 million. That amount is divided among the players, and the amount they receive depends on the last round they won.

The tournament in Mexico was on a hard court. My opponent was a girl from Peru, Rosa-Maria Mendoza. Surprisingly, I was up four–1 quickly, winning the first set six–1. It happened so fast—maybe thirty to thirty-five minutes, which is very quick in tennis.

I could hardly believe I'd won my first set of the match. Unfortunately, the realization got my mind wandering. I started imagining winning, and with tennis being such a mental game, my distracted thoughts affected my playing. This is what happens when you get in your head—you play tight, and the other player senses your nervousness and gains momentum against you. Rosa could probably sense my distraction, but despite being in my head, I still managed to win the second set six–0.

Winning that match was a tremendous relief. I was awarded my first pro points. Most of Percy's players had pro points. For me, winning validated my inclusion in that elite group. That tournament showed me I could not only play professionally but win too. Pro points mattered.

A player's ranking is based on points, which differ based on the tournament level and the rounds won. Winning a match in that tournament was worth one point, giving me my first professional ranking. I was fourteen—the youngest a tennis player may play professionally. In tennis, fourteen-year-olds are considered adult players. That set me up to play against other professional fourteen-year-olds and pros as old as thirty-six. Basically fourteen was the youngest you could be, but you could play against a woman of any age on the other side of the court as long as she was fourteen or older.

I thought that was strange, but I accepted it. In boxing, there are weight classes so people of vastly different builds don't compete against each other. In tennis, a scrawny teenager could compete against a muscled adult woman.

Winning that match was also the first time I got paid to play tennis. However, accepting money for my sport would have classified me as a pro, and I'd then lose my eligibility to play college sports on a scholarship. So I could only accept enough of the earnings to cover my expenses, a loophole that many tennis players relied on. My Mexico win helped pay for my flight, hotel, and meals. This NIL (name, image, and likeness) rule changed over the years, and now college players can get paid to play.

In pro tournaments, the player gets a rest day between matches. Two days after winning against Rosa, I played Valeria Pulido Velasco, one of the highest-ranked girls in Mexico. A huge crowd showed up to support their home country star, and Valeria beat me, six–2, six–3.

I felt like Rosa must have felt when I beat her, maybe worse. That was my first time playing against someone that big in their home country. I got a taste of what it's like to play when the entire crowd's against you. When you're in that situation, people don't just want you to lose; they want to see their player demolish you. Depending on the country and the crowd, they might yell insults at you and call you names. Sometimes they throw things onto the court. At times the umpires will make calls against you because they want their home player to win and they feel the pressure from the crowd. Losing to Valeria wasn't too awful, but I would have some dreadful experiences later in my career competing against hometown girls. Still, that loss showed me I couldn't rest on my laurels. There was more work to do if I was going to be taken seriously as a professional tennis player.

STRATEGIES FOR WINNING

To win, I had to stay focused. I avoided looking at other people in the stands, especially when they were against me. I'd seen what could happen to a player affected by an unfriendly crowd. When your opponent gets frustrated, you think, *Yes, it's getting to them!* This is the game within the game that most people don't notice, but to the players, it's everything. Once a player is distracted or upset, they lose their momentum, and the energy shifts. You can feel the player failing, or "choking," as the pressure gets to them. They usually try to maintain their composure, but it's still happening.

Whether I won or lost a point, I stuck to my routine: looking at my racket, playing with my strings, and breathing a certain way. Whether the audience was screaming at me to lose or cheering me on, I stuck to my routine. Allowing the other player or the audience to affect me could be a distraction. Occasionally, I'd look at my parents, but only when I made a great shot or won a big point. Playing in other countries, my mom and dad weren't hard to find because our box was so small. They were the only two people in the crowd who wanted me to win!

Likewise, I was conscious of my emotions on the court. If I lost a point, I did my best not to react. If I got an easy point, I didn't react. If I made a really long point or had a really nice winner, I might holler "Come on!" or "Let's go!" but I never overreacted. Remaining stoic inside and out mattered. I focused on my breathing, my racket, the moment, and the game, and didn't dwell on whatever had just happened. That was the past, and I had to stay present to win. That meant ignoring everything else—the people, the points, and especially my opponent, staring me down over the net.

Every two games, players switch sides on the court. During the switch, there's a ninety-second break for rest and water. You have to cross your opponent to get to the other side. This is also an important moment. Do you ignore them? Look them in the eye? Give them a shoulder? None of this is accidental. The exchange can be cordial, or it can be rough, depending on the players' histories and how the game is going.

In this way, tennis is sort of like poker or chess. People who know tennis might pick up on these tiny details that the average fan misses. For instance, if a player loses a set and immediately takes a bathroom break, chances are, they're using that time to refresh themselves by changing clothes and giving themselves a pep talk. Bathroom breaks aren't always fair. If you play against someone in their country, expect them to get longer breaks. Meanwhile, the winning player loses their momentum. Winning players want to keep moving quickly. Losers want to slow the game down. If they slow it down too much, they can get a penalty. So players practice slowing down the game just enough to give themselves time to evaluate what's going on and how they can claw their way back without getting into trouble with the ref.

ANOTHER AWARD

In 2008, I'd been living on the IMG campus for eight years. The academy held its end-of-year banquet for students who lived on the campus, which was different from the one for the tennis program. Students from every sport and their parents attended. Various awards were given out, and just like when I won the one hundred Percent Effort award, I didn't expect any kind of recognition at the event. Again, I was caught off guard when they called my name. The Academy gave me the Longevity Award for living on campus longer than any student in IMG history.

7

THE DECISION

I stopped working with Nick Bollettieri. Not because he wasn't a brilliant coach. He was the best. But as an up-and-coming junior tournament player with promise, to bolster my credibility as a serious contender, I needed a coach who was active in the current professional space. My dad hired Coach Ales Kodat from the Czech Republic, who was the stepfather and current coach of former top-ten player Nicole Vaidišová.

Nicole was a pro signed by IMG. She was a great player, but an emotional player, too—the stereotypical tennis pro whose moods swung wildly with the game. As long as she was playing well, she was unbeatable. The minute the tide turned against her, Nicole became upset and passionate about the situation she was in. Often, if she lost a point or wasn't happy about how she played the point, she appeared to take out her frustration on Ales in the player's box, glaring and even screaming obscenities. He always remained so poised and calm.

Despite her temper, Nicole was someone I aspired to be like at the Academy. She was tall, like me, standing five feet eleven. She had a massive wingspan and a huge serve. For being so tall, she moved pretty well too. I looked up to her as a player because at such a young age she had already achieved some incredible things. In 2007, at the young age of seventeen, she became the twelfth-youngest player in WTA history to achieve a top-ten ranking. What is so wild is that she announced her retirement just a few short years after this, in 2010, citing a "lack of interest." Because she achieved so much so quickly and worked so hard and made so much money, I could see why after experiencing some tough losses she would not want to keep playing. The WTA tour is a total grind, and back then the players were not friends. It was not a fun environment. It was like the Hunger Games every week.

Nicole's exit from tennis worked in my favor; when she took a break from tennis to deal with personal issues, her stepdad, Coach Ales, became available to coach other players. My parents liked Ales partly because Nicole and I had similar builds. We were about the same height and played with similar styles. At first, Ales wasn't keen on coaching me. He'd been working with Nicole at the highest levels tennis had to offer, while I was still trying to make a name for myself. Coaches have egos and reputations to protect. He would have been basically starting over, working with me. I was a solid player at number eighty-five in the world in the ITF juniors; Nicole was in the top five in juniors before becoming a standout pro. The level and clout was different and Ales had to weigh all the pros and cons. Somehow, my dad convinced him to give me a shot, and I started training with him daily. Everything changed for me.

BEING COACHED BY ALES

My old coach, Nick, constantly gave me feedback on my performance. He corrected me when I played poorly and boosted my self-esteem with praise when I played well.

Ales's Eastern European style of coaching was the opposite. There was no consistent praise. Ales was all about technique and the fundamentals. He told me what he wanted, and I tried my best to emulate it. There was no feedback. At first, I thought he was mad at me. It was night and day from working with Nick, Jimmy, and every other coach I'd had up until that point. They were constantly talking and reinforcing. This was so different. Why didn't he say anything other than give instruction? For me, that was a big adjustment.

Ales was extremely technical about everything, including foot placement. He showed me how to hit in new ways and how to move my feet in a sort of figure-eight pattern I'd never seen before. He really loved the open stance style of play that includes footwork different from hitting closed stance, where your body is more closed off and you turn your hips and shoulders into the ball, sort of the way baseball players stand to hit a ball. Learning to move around the court in the figure-eights and also to be hitting mostly open stance was a massive adjustment. It was like learning to play tennis from scratch. I'd look to my parents on the sidelines, questioning this new approach. Initially, I felt like I was regressing. At home, they told me to trust the process. Ales had coached Nicole, and she was one of the top players in the world. I never doubted what Ales was teaching me. He knew what it took to be the best in the world. I more questioned myself and whether I could learn and pick up the new footwork.

At first, I struggled. Ales corrected me each time, and as I tweaked my movements and got closer to what he wanted, my tennis improved. It was different. It was wild. And it worked! Over time, I started getting an occasional "good job" or "nice!" I came to appreciate Ales's style because when he complimented me, I knew it meant something.

Ales started traveling around the world with me to professional tournaments. That was an enormous change—traveling with a coach instead of my parents. I'd gone to a junior tournament with a coach years earlier, but this was different. We went to Europe for a month. It was a long time to be with a very serious guy whose only focus was tennis and who didn't do small talk. The trip was all business—all tennis, all the time. I realized it must have been a huge adjustment for Ales as well, traveling out of the country without his family. He had a wife and children in the States, so this was just as much a sacrifice for him as for me.

Just like on the tennis court, Ales didn't talk a lot during meals. Part of this was due to his personality, but he was also less talkative, I believe, because English was not his native language. This was before people pulled out their phones to check social media and surf the web during meals. I was a teenager, and with no one at the table to talk to, I learned to enjoy my food more and take in my surroundings. I became more observant. I started watching people more. That month, I learned to sit in stillness and silence and be okay. I learned to enjoy a meal with a person and not speak, to be around people without saying a word. For a social extrovert like me, that was new, and an important lesson I carry with me to this day. Being uncomfortable was also good for me. I realized that the most awkward times for me offered the greatest opportunity for growth.

I traveled all over with Ales. Playing in Norway, Sweden, and Denmark showed me what it was like to play in countries with twenty-four hours of daylight or darkness, depending on the season. I played there during the summer months, and I had to get used to the sun being out in the middle of the night. The hotels had blackout shades on all the windows so guests could sleep.

I saw Ales open up once. We were in Norway for a tournament, and I was playing doubles with a girl from the Czech Republic, Kateřina Kramperová, who became my friend. Her coach was also Czech, and he and Ales had lively conversations. They would laugh and joke and go on walks together. I had no idea what they talked about, but I was happy for my coach. Wi-Fi wasn't as prevalent as it is today, so Ales and the other coach spent their downtime playing cards and board games. It was the first time I saw my coach laugh and actually have fun.

I spent my downtime trying to learn Czech. Picking up new languages was a habit I developed early on. Even knowing a few phrases helped me connect with people from other countries quickly. When people saw me trying to speak in their native language, they encouraged me and were willing to teach me more. This became such an important skill in my life. When I learned a few phrases in languages that nobody expected me to know, people seemed to have a deeper respect for my effort. As a mixed girl speaking some Czech, you had best believe I received some attention and praise, especially if I could get the accent down correctly. I could often do this, as accents seem to come naturally to me. I loved being authentic in each new language. I still have a pet peeve for Americans who learn a new language but speak with an overexaggerated American accent. That automatically gives away where they are from.

PLAYING IN MELILLA WITH COACH ALES

I played some of my best tennis in a $10,000 singles tournament on the Spanish island of Melilla, located off the coast of Africa. Even though I didn't win the finals, I won every match leading up to it. Everything Coach Ales taught me came into play, and I was clicking. I won two three-set matches, playing against girls with higher rankings earlier in the tournament. This was a true testament to the growth I'd developed working with Ales. Up until that point, I hadn't won many three-set matches, especially where I had won the first match and lost the second. In the past, that momentum swing would have brought me down mentally, and I would have lost the third set, still "butt hurt" from losing the second. During this tournament, I not only won three-set matches, but I was also the one doing the momentum changing, winning the second and third sets. I'd won doubles tournaments in the past, but this was my best performance in a professional singles tournament. My parents weren't there to see it, and back then, coaches weren't allowed to instruct players during matches. So I felt like it was just me and my thoughts on the court—along with everything my coaches, and especially Ales, had taught me, and with the trust that my parents had placed in him.

I can still remember some of my thoughts during those matches. Time seemed to slow down but also fly by. I felt like I was in the zone, which is a feeling athletes experience when everything is going right for them and they don't have to think about what they are doing. It just happens. I felt like I belonged there too. Even though I was a teenager, the other players were women, traveling with their coaches while their parents stayed behind. For the first time, I felt like a pro.

DAD FINDS TOURNAMENTS

My father tracked all the pro tournaments. He especially looked for days when more than one tournament was scheduled. Players would have to pick one, which meant opportunities for me to squeeze in as a wild card at tournaments where major players had to play some-where else and there weren't enough opponents. If a tournament had a sixty-four-player draw and the top players were stretched between two or three tournaments around the world, this would cause the tournament to have some additional openings for players who wouldn't typically get into a tournament of this level and cal-iber on their own. Dad sent me to these tournaments, and I didn't always get to play. Sometimes, the risks paid off, like when I played in the Rogers Cup—twice! I also played in the Cincinnati Open, then called the Western & Southern Open. The Cincinnati Open is one of the ATP Masters 1000 tournaments on the ATP Tour and one of the WTA 1000 tournaments on the WTA Tour. It's the third largest tennis event in the United States, after the US Open and the Indian Wells Open. A major tournament leading up to the US Open, the Western & Southern's prize money was around $2 million, maybe less, compared to about double that for the US Open. Still, it was a lot of money. At about five hundred in the world, I wouldn't typically be eligible to play in a tournament like the Cincinnati Open. These were Serena- and Venus-level players, not Danielle-level players. They were among the top fifty or so girls in the world.

I got in with a wild card opening, and Ales and my parents flew to Ohio with me. I was excited to play, but I was also happy for Ales. This was the kind of tournament he usually attended with Nicole. He was used to having his hotel comped and being chauffeured around in a player car. This was the major leagues of tennis, a lavish world he'd enjoyed before taking me on as a client. Now, I would be on the biggest stage of my career, and I was taking Ales with me.

In the locker room, the names of players I idolized were written on locker tags. Freaking out on the inside, I kept my composure and pretended it was just another day, just another tournament. My opponent was Sorana Mihaela Cîrstea, a top junior girl from Romania who went on to achieve a singles ranking of twenty-one in the world.

We played on the largest stadium court, the grandstand court. I knew this would be one of the hardest matches of my life, and I had never been so nervous to step onto a tennis court. However, there was no pressure on me to win. The pressure was all on Sorana. If I lost a game, she'd look bad. I'd just look like I was supposed to look—not as good as one of the top players.

Thoughts flew through my mind. *What if...?* What if I actually won a game? What if I won the match? Unlikely, but those "what if" moments are unavoidable. The possibility was mind-blowing. Winning would be life changing. My parents were there, of course. My dad wouldn't have missed his daughter playing against a top player in a major tournament for anything.

Before the match, during our five-minute warm-up, I couldn't believe how fast Sorana was. How hard she hit that ball! This was a whole new level of tennis for me. I had to adjust quickly because that tennis ball would come back at me harder and faster than I was accustomed to.

I didn't win the match—but I didn't get "bageled" either, meaning I didn't lose six–o, six–o. I actually won a few games. I won money, too, around $20,000. That was the most I'd ever been paid to play tennis at that time, and I didn't even win the tournament! In past tournaments I'd played, even the top winner came away with, at best, around $2,000. Of course, I couldn't accept it all, only enough to cover my expenses.

My mind was spinning after that tournament. I'd had a taste of what it was like to play with a top player at the top level, on a stadium court in front of thousands of people, and get paid well for it. If I could only get enough professional points to play at tournaments like the Cincinnati all the time. That was my goal.

Dad got me into a handful of tournaments like that over the years. They were golden moments that kept the dream alive. If I could win one, everything would change. Without his looking out for me, campaigning for me, doing everything within his power to get me to the biggest tennis stages he could find, those moments wouldn't have happened. I'll always be grateful to him for giving me those chances, those experiences. Not every sports parent does that for their kid.

CAMPAIGNING FOR DANIELLE

Over time, I learned to campaign for myself. Like my dad, I became strategic about my career. Opportunities seldom fall into a person's lap—you have to go out there and find them. Take risks, too, because no matter how well you plan, your hard work might not pay off.

I didn't have an agent, and I wasn't big enough for sponsors to pursue me. I had to go after them. If I wanted the racket company Yonex and the tennis footwear and apparel company K-Swiss to see me, I had to pitch myself. So I worked on my speaking and my photos, and I reached out to both companies with proposals. This was before AI and ChatGPT could make my emails and documents look perfect. Would they sponsor an up-and-coming player? They agreed, and I was delighted. The work didn't stop there because once sponsored, I had to represent those companies. I was up for all of it. This was what I wanted, what I had been working toward. Getting those sponsorships proved to me I didn't have to wait for good things to come to me. I could make my own opportunities. I could look at myself in the mirror, wearing K-Swiss clothing, a Yonex racket in hand, and say, "You were the afterthought, Danielle—the girl in the next-to-worst group who would not amount to anything. Look at where you are now."

A MAJOR DECISION

In 2009, during my senior year of high school, I faced a pivotal choice: go to college or continue to play pro. That I was playing the best tennis of my life made the choice more difficult. I had a great coach and was making gains. Going pro meant playing year-round, and I wondered how far I could go at that pace. The temptation to continue playing was powerful, tempered only by the games I didn't win. Going to college meant playing pro only three months of the year, with the other months devoted to playing college tennis. Back then, players had to make a definitive choice. They couldn't be college students and full-time pro athletes.[4]

College was a tempting choice too. I'd get a scholarship and a full ride, with no student debt to pay off. If tennis didn't play out for me the way I hoped, I'd have an education to fall back on.

Another wrinkle was that I was living with my parents during my senior year. That meant more restrictions. I felt as if I had regressed, going from the relative freedom of the IMG campus to being twelve again, under my parents' watchful eyes. They wanted to know where I was every minute. Even though I had a car, they told me when to go, where to go, and when to stay home. After traveling the world with my coach and being treated like an adult, the limits to my independence were painful. They'd continue if I played pro because until I was able to support myself, I'd still be living under their roof. College looked like true adult freedom.

My parents wanted me to go pro. They were committed to supporting the dream of me going all the way until it happened. Part of me—a big part—wanted that too. I was still just ranked among the top 500s of the world WTA, but all it took was one big tournament to put me on the map. Other girls from Percy's group were already doing it, moving up to the 200s. One girl, Michelle Larcher de Brito, was among the top one hundred. I had to be honest with myself. Did I have what it took to be as good as the other girls? I always tell people not to compare themselves with others. It's not healthy and accomplishes nothing. Yet in this situation, I couldn't help comparing myself to the girls in Percy's group.

Ultimately, my desire for freedom won out. I couldn't continue living at home—not for another year, and definitely not for years to come. My tennis career was anyone's guess. College—my ticket to being on my own and answering to no one—was a sure bet.

My parents weren't thrilled with my decision, but they didn't fight it. They weren't delusional about my abilities. They believed in me, but they also wanted whatever was best for my future. I'd continue playing pro during the summer and fall, so it wasn't like I was giving up on our pro dreams altogether. All it took was one win, one tournament, and everything could change.

WHERE TO GO TO SCHOOL

Hundreds of colleges had sent me letters wanting me to attend their university, and I'd been putting them all aside. Once I'd decided to pursue an education, I had to wade through them. My dad had a folder for everything, and he organized and documented everything. My next major decision was choosing a school that made the most sense for my future.

The University of Miami was my first choice. Unlike the small town of Bradenton, where IMG was located, Miami was the best Florida had to offer. The beaches, the clubs, the people. The *lifestyle*. Miami fit my personality to a T. I loved dancing. Loved going to parties. Seldom got to do either, and I yearned for a change. Miami had everything I wanted. It wasn't a typical "college town," where the whole place revolved around the school. It was a big, vibrant city that had a great university.

As if the lifestyle, location, and climate weren't enough to tempt me, another tennis player I knew from traveling and tournaments,

Julia Cohen, was there already. Julia was a high-ranked junior player who also played pro, like me. She was at the university and said I should go there too. That made up my mind: I was going to the University of Miami.

OPERATION GET DANIELLE INTO SCHOOL

As much as I wanted the University of Miami (and it wanted me), one obstacle stood in the way: my SAT scores were horrible. When I was at IMG, the educational program wasn't my focus. The focus changed over the years, and now the school prides itself on turning out well-rounded, college-ready people instead of just outstanding athletes. Graduates are more prepared for continuing their education and building successful careers outside the sports world. However, when I was a student at Pendleton, academics weren't important to IMG, my parents, or me. Now that I was trying to get into college, academics were everything.

Suddenly, my focus, and my parents', went from "school isn't a big deal" to "school matters and you'd better get those scores up pronto." My math scores were the problem, so my parents hired a tutor, Mark Riddell. Mark worked for Scott Tribley, who my parents had hired to guide me through the college admission process.

I worked with the tutor, studied, tested, and failed. On my fourth try, my scores were acceptable for the University of Miami. I breathed a huge sigh of relief and finally accepted the scholarship.

Years later, Mark became notorious for his role in "Operation Varsity Blues," a scandal involving wealthy parents paying to have their kids bypass the usual college admission requirements. Apparently, my parents were never approached with this kind of deal. They wouldn't have entertained cheating anyway. I had to work for everything. My parents demanded it. I took the SAT *four times*. Math!

MY FIRST BOYFRIEND, SORT OF

In my senior year of high school, I finally had a boyfriend. My mother sort of knew about him, but I kept Alex a secret from my dad. A soccer player, Alex joined IMG after graduating from high school. He wasn't getting the attention he needed to play Division I college ball, and a year at IMG could be just enough to make the difference. Alex wasn't the only student who came to IMG after high school. A lot of kids did that, and for the same reason: they were really good, but not quite good enough to get a sports scholarship. Or they got offers, but not from top colleges.

Did I mention I was a rule-follower? Alex was not. He liked to party. After turning down numerous offers to join him for nights out on the town, I finally caved, snuck out of the house, and went to a party.

In my house, sneaking out was a major deal. The whole house was wired to an alarm system. My bedroom window had a lock on the inside, and if I left my room, my parents were alerted. Any security breach was recorded by the alarm system.

Sometimes, I noticed, they forgot to set it. Other nights, they set it but didn't check to see if there were any windows or doors left ajar. I started leaving my window cracked open a bit to see if they noticed. If they asked about it, I'd say I wanted some fresh air. When they didn't mention it, I figured my window was a safe option for getting away at night.

On the night of the party, I squeezed out the window. Slowly, I lowered it behind me, leaving it open just a notch so I could get back in. In the dark of night, I hurried down the street and into the waiting car of friends. I was off to the party! As scary as it was, the feeling was also exhilarating. I was out on my own without my parents' permission.

The feeling didn't last. No sooner did I arrive at the party when my phone started going off. It was my dad. He must have called me thirty times, and I was afraid to answer. My friends, including Alex, told me to answer the phone, but I couldn't. I'd never been in trouble. I didn't break rules, and I didn't know what would happen to me.

I wasn't prepared to speak to my father, but I knew I had to go home. Alex dropped me off a few houses down from my parents' home so I could get my bearings. I needed to walk, to breathe, before facing my father. Who knew what I was walking into?

My parents were sitting on the couch. They motioned for me to sit between them. Terrified, I took my place and waited for my punishment. Weirdly, no one yelled. Mom didn't say a word. Dad spoke in a low tone, not angrily, but in a way that made me feel like the worst person in the world.

"You left a window open," he said, "and endangered the whole family. Anyone could have come into the house. We could have been killed." My father went on like that for a long time. I wanted him to yell, to scream at me for sneaking out when I knew it was against the rules. His rules. Instead, he went on and on, putting me on the biggest guilt trip until I just wanted to sink into the couch and disappear.

The funny thing was, he never asked where I went or what I did. I don't think he wanted to know. My father has always seen me as a precious child, and he never allowed anything to mar that image. If he had asked, I would have told him exactly what happened: absolutely nothing. I didn't drink at the party, or do drugs, or mess around with any boys. I didn't even have fun. I spent a whole twenty minutes being petrified of coming home. For days after that night, I focused on one thing: *two more months, and I'm leaving for Miami.*

WHY I CHOSE THE UNIVERSITY OF MIAMI

I chose Miami for a lot of reasons. I didn't want to go to college in the northern United States because I'd be playing on indoor courts most of the year. In Florida, I could continue playing outside year-round. It wasn't so much that playing outside was easier—it wasn't. Indoor courts were climate-controlled, so people who played on them all the time often struggled to play outside, where the wind, weather, temperature, and humidity varied. I wanted to maintain all the training I'd had so far, which included knowing how to adjust to the outside environment.

If the location wasn't enough to convince me, the coach was. Coach Caroline said all the right things.

"The team here is very international, and I've developed a lot of students who play professionally," she said. Most importantly, she said I would only have to play for the college during the spring, their regular team season. For the rest of the year, while other student athletes played individually to help boost their NCAA ratings, I'd be free to travel and play professionally in tournaments. It sounded too good to be true.

The IMG coaches had mixed opinions about my decision to go to college. Most of them supported me. They knew the odds of anyone making it as a professional athlete were slim. They'd seen students take that path. Some made it. Some didn't. Of those who didn't, some fell apart. They'd dedicated their lives to the single goal of becoming a professional athlete, and when they didn't make it, they felt worthless, like their lives had been a complete waste of time. Some players made a lot of money and then lost it all. Others turned to drugs and alcohol. Still others turned to coaching.

Coaching tennis might sound like an awesome career, but when you're shooting for the stars, it's the last thing you want to do. For many, that was their only choice. With no skills other than their sport, they had no other options.

Imagine being twenty-eight years young. You've been playing tennis since you could hold a racket. It's all you know. With no college and no work experience, what kind of job opportunities do you have to look forward to? It's a terrifying situation that tennis players and other athletes often have to face.

The IMG coaches knew all this. Unless a player had extraordinary talent, they didn't talk them out of college. It was better to play Division I tennis and then have a successful career than to struggle through years of mediocre tennis and have nothing to show for it.

Ales wanted me to pursue a professional tennis career. He believed I had the potential to make it.

PROM NIGHT

My relationship with Alex fizzled out soon after the party. For my senior prom, I went with a golfer from Korea named Tae Kim. We were friends, not romantic. Tae was outgoing and a lot of fun to be around. He was taller than I was too. For some reason, I had always believed Asian people were petite. That wasn't true of Asian athletes. IMG students from China and Korea were all very tall.

Tae and I, along with some friends, rented a limo for the night. I hung out with everybody for an hour and a half after the prom, but then I had to be home while everyone else stuck around. The prom, and the hour and a half after, were special, though. I felt normal, like just another teenager, and it felt good. If college was anything like that night, my life was about to get a lot better.

Barion Mills and Danielle as a baby.

Danielle as a baby with Barion Mills.

Barion Mills and Danielle at one year old on vacation.

Danielle almost two years old with a tennis ball, while Barion is hitting on the wall in Athena High School Park in Rochester, Greece, New York.

Danielle as a toddler.

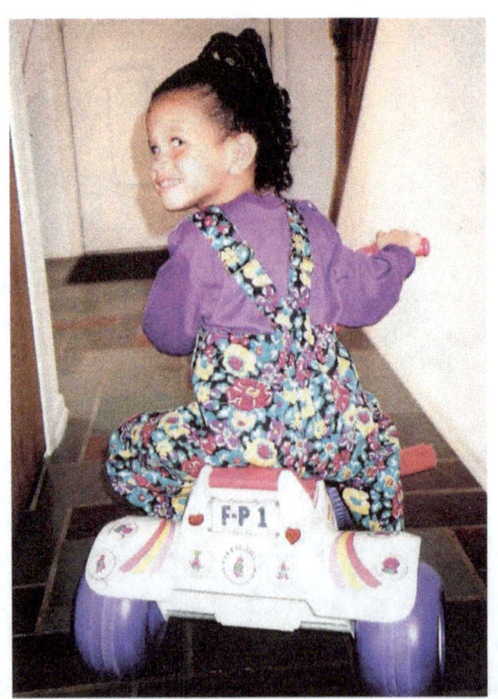

Danielle at three or four years old after getting her hair done.

Danielle in a tennis clinic at five years old at Midtown Athletic Club in Rochester, New York.

Danielle at four years old with long hair.

Danielle at eight or nine years old working at her mom's insurance agency, Insurance Direct (helping to scan policies).

Danielle and her dad Barion Mills in Rochester, New York, at his agency.

Norma and Barion Mills early on at their agency after college.

Danielle with Nick Bollettieri during Summer Camp, eleven years old, 2001.

Serena Williams and Danielle Mills at eleven years old at IMG.

Danielle with Nick Bollettieri on the famous steps outside of Nick's court.

Danielle and Nick Bollettieri talking on the stairs by Nick's court on Court one. She's around thirteen years old.

Danielle and Nick Bollettieri training on the original indoor courts.

Danielle at eleven years old at IMG with a Nick Bollettieri
water jug and her Head racket bag.

Danielle at ninety-seven pounds and wearing a "cat
suit," hitting with Jimmy on Court three.

Danielle with her first tennis coach Ron Dyson and current coach
Nick Bollettieri at IMG Academy in Rochester, New York.

Danielle at around thirteen years old hitting a serve on Nick's
court with Nick, Jimmy Nagelsen, and Greg Hill looking on.

Original Percy's Group—Mary Clayton, Danielle, Tammy Hendler, Percy Melzi, Jordanne Dobbins, Michelle Larcher de Brito, Nicole Bartnik, Tara Moore.

Danielle with Pat Etcheberry, "The Serve Doctor," training at IMG.

Danielle with WTA pro Daniela Hantuchová at the
Miami Open in Key Biscayne, Florida.

Danielle with Jennifer Capriati at IMG when Danielle was twelve.

Academy Pamphlet.

The Full-Time Program

20 Top 10 Players in 20 Years

Maria Sharapova: 2004 Wimbledon Women's Singles Champion. *Currently ranked Top Ten in the world. Maria has won six WTA events and currently trains at NBTA.*

- Our Full-time students have won 33 Grand Slams.
- Over 95% of our 2004 college bound seniors received college scholarship assistance.
- Our success comes from the size of our program— over 200 players. We create a high level of daily competition for all ages and abilities.
- Our philosophy is to produce champions on and off the court.
- Full-time students learn the value of discipline, commitment, sacrifice, responsibility, competition (winning & losing), goal setting and goal achieving.
- We offer Boarding & Non-boarding options.
- Students who have graduated high school can train all day.
- We offer a choice of three Accredited schools with curriculums delivered around our tennis program. Students graduate from Pendleton, Bradenton Academy or St. Stephens and attend some of the best colleges in the USA.
- Our full-time program runs from September through May.
- Inquire today to reserve your place in the full-time program and experience the Bollettieri tradition of excellence.

Summer Camp

"The Toughest Playground in the World"

- Summer Camp dates: June - August every year.
- All ability levels from 8 to 18 years are welcome.
- Arrive Sunday - Depart Saturday.
- Three-week training blocks produce optimal results

Train like the Pros each day:

- 3 hours of stroke production/training (drilling).
- 1 hour of physical conditioning (IPI).
- 2 hours of matchplay.
- 1 hour of mental conditioning or training in the Strategy Zone each week.

Program Features:

- Video Analysis of strokes.
- Video and Strategy Zone analysis of matches.
- Florida tournaments on some weekends.
- Trips to Disney World, Islands of Adventure, Universal Studios, Sea World, Busch Gardens and much more are scheduled on some weekends.

It's more than a Summer Camp—it's an Experience!
There are two kinds of players — the ones who have been to Bollettieri's and the ones who haven't...yet!

Call Today and become a part of the Bollettieri Team!

Note: July and August sell out quickly, so be sure to make reservations early.

Academy Brochure with Danielle hitting a volley next to Michelle Larcher de Brito.

Danielle on IMG campus with Jessica and Gabriela.

Danielle at Nick's annual alumni event in 2025—Jimmy Arias,
Juan Herrera, Danielle, Margie Zesinger, Mary Pierce.

Danielle and Javier Walden for their engagement photos.

Danielle playing at the Rogers Coupe in Montreal, Canada.

Danielle moderating panel at Miami Open event
with Monica Puig and Jennifer Brady.

Barion Mills holding up his book, Stress-Free Success, and
Danielle's first book, How to Master LinkedIn.

Danielle speaking on a panel for Black Sports Professionals annual Juneteenth Event, 2024.

Danielle on court with Nick and Michelle Larcher de Brito.

Nick Bollettieri talking with Danielle's parents, Barion
and Norma Mills, during a practice.

Danielle on Nick's court practicing.

Danielle practicing with Nick. You can see him with his shirt off getting a tan.

Danielle giving the opening keynote at a conference in 2023.

Danielle and Jah Walden at Miami Swim Week.

Danielle and Jah Walden at Miami Swim Week.

Danielle and Jah at the Versace Mansion in Miami Beach, Florida.

Danielle hosting the Digital Dealer Conference in Las Vegas in 2013.

Barion Mills playing at IMG Academy.

Danielle and Coach Julio Moros.

Danielle with the female tennis program at IMG after
Margie invited her to speak to the girls.

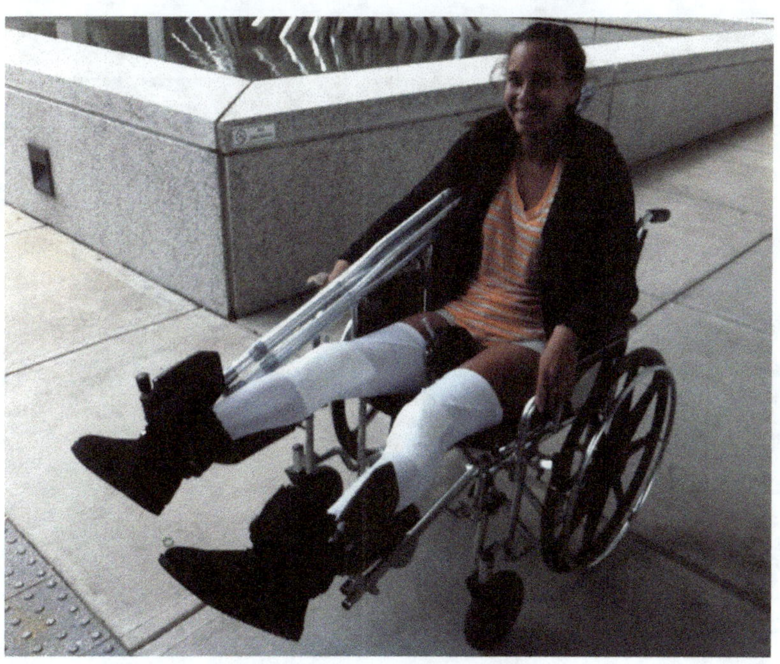

Danielle after her double knee surgery.

Danielle with Jimmy Nagelsen on Court three putting in the hours on the court.

Ron Dyson with Danielle and Nick.

Danielle and Norma during Danielle and Norma's time during the summer program, when Danielle attended for a week and Norma also attended for a week.

Danielle with her 2011 BMW 1 series. This was her third vehicle.

To Mills Family
From Nick Bollettieri   Jan. 27-2004

    I have given thought to the
input for the Development of your
daughter (Danielle)
    All of us involved including the
very positive work Jimmy has done
along with Julio is truly rewarding
for only 1 year
    The Development of a young player
should have a specific plan for each
player keeping in mind everyone is
very different
    We must find what is Best
for Danielle
    In order to do this there is a
great deal of research to do including
① Danielle's Goals
② Her Physical make-up
③ Foot Speed & Agility
④ How Does she practice
⑤ Court Stratgey (Very Imp.)
We may have to get Lance more
involved in not only her court
play including stats

Letter from Nick Bollettieri to Danielle's parents discussing her play and goals.

10) PArents expectatinis, support
and opinion ABout my plan
(B)
6) WHAt type of Coach Dres she
re-act to
7) Does she speak up
8) How Does she re-act to the
UNKNOWN
9) Can she recognize the strengths
and weakness of her opponent and
then Know How to make Adjustme

TechNiques
It is my job to evaulate
each stroke and then determine
what must Be Done

Note
It is imperative we take Advan
Being a lefty and accept the
fact she must develope a Big
Serve

Nick Input

I will Work with Jimmy
making sure we are Both on the
same page
He should be part of some of
my lessons which then will
avoid Confusion

Letter from Nick Bollettieri to Danielle's parents discussing her play and goals.

PLAN e Cost

During the months of Feb—March
April - May I will personally
work with her when I am in
residence

In my ABSENCE I will set up
a lesson plan for Jimy to follow
when he gives her lessons.

I also will have Julio, Greg,
HASSAN and Jimy Be paid by me
of my lessons so they can continue
the same plan of Action for Daniell

Cost
20,00

You can pay this in Two
payments

Feb 1st   10,00

April 1st   10,00

Letter from Nick Bollettieri to Danielle's parents discussing her play and goals.

Danielle back at IMG's Mind Gym, which is in a new location, but it's where her mindset was built.

Danielle with Nenad Cacic and Mary Pierce at the Nick Bollettieri alumni event in 2025.

Danielle with Sabine Lisicki and Margie Zesinger at Nick's alumni event in 2025.

Danielle with Eddy Kranjcevic, Tommy Haas, and
Danielle Bollettieri at Nick's alumni event.

Danielle hitting with Cedrik Stebe, Sabine Lisicki, Coach
Eddy Kranjcevic, and Nenad Cacic.

Danielle after a photoshoot in Miami.

Danielle on Court one with Nick.

Danielle and Dwight Powell back at IMG.

Danielle practicing. You can see how strong she was.

Danielle signing autographs at the Rogers Coupe.

Danielle signing autographs at the Family Circle Cup in Charleston, South Carolina.

Danielle being interviewed at the Grant Cardone 10X Growth Conference.

Danielle and Javier's wedding day with their wedding party.

Danielle and Jah (Javier) on their wedding day.

Barion and Danielle at the Citi Open, where Barion is providing on-court coaching.

Danielle against Naomi Osaka in Irapuato, Mexico, 2014.

Danielle training with Coach Margie on Nick's court.

Danielle with Margie Zesinger out at dinner when Danielle was in high school.

Danielle hosting the annual Upstart Live All Company
Conference while pregnant, 2024.

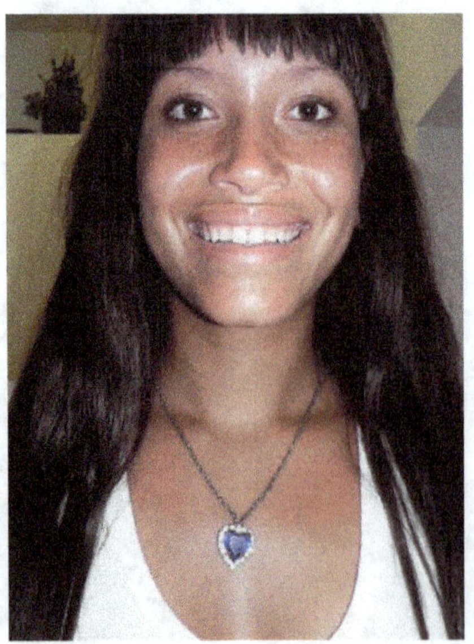

A young Danielle early on at IMG 2002.

Carolina Murphy's memorial after her thirty-seven years of service at IMG. This is the woman who interviewed Danielle to live on campus back in 2001.

Danielle with Freddy Adu.

The 2010 University of Miami tennis team with Cameron Diaz.

Danielle hitting a volley during her freshman year at the University of Miami, with her teammates watching.

Danielle and Margie out for dinner in Sarasota, Florida, 2009.

Danielle's college dorm room with all the fashion magazine photos as wallpaper.

Danielle's college dorm room with all the fashion magazine photos as wallpaper.

Danielle and Nicole Bartnik at a pro tournament in Captiva Island, Florida.

Danielle with Shelly Summers in 2009, when they learned
they both would be going to the University of Miami.

Danielle with Madison Brengle, Michelle Larcher de Brito, Nicole Vaidišová, and Tammy (Hendler) Emmrich.

Danielle mid volley at $50k in Fort Worth, Texas, 2013.

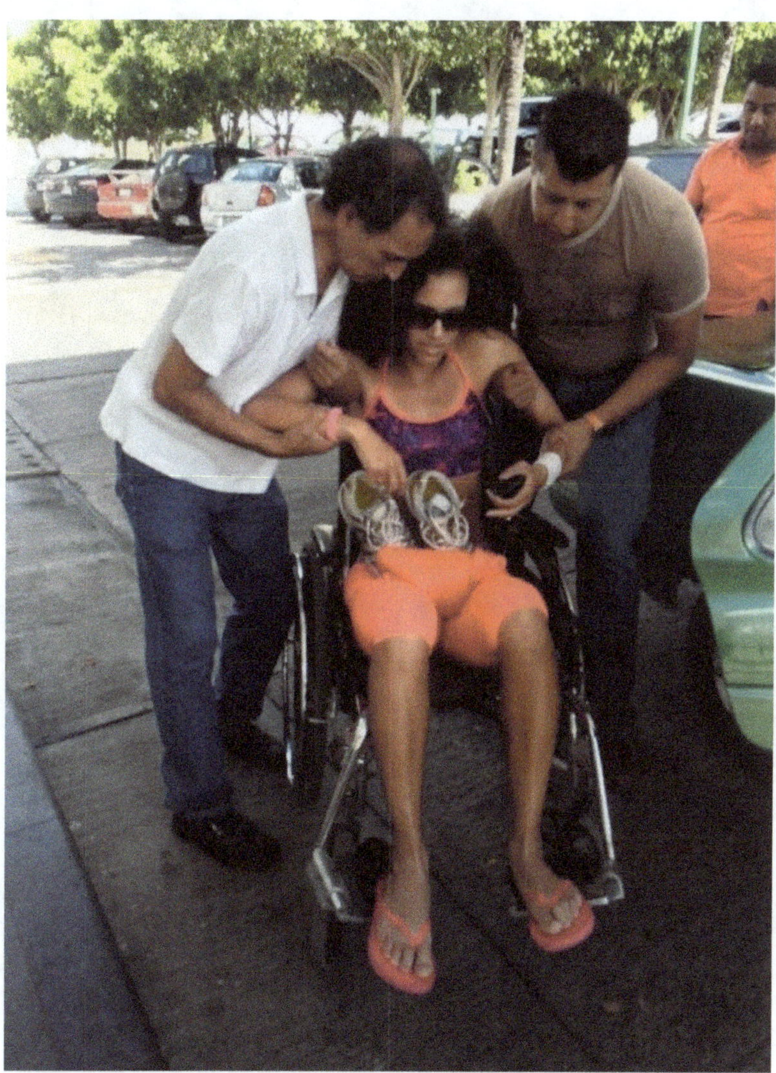

Danielle being helped into the taxi in San Luis Potosi, Mexico, after she herniated two discs in her back, L4 and L5.

PART II

GOING PRO

8

THE UNIVERSITY OF MIAMI

Being home felt like being in jail. I had no freedom, or what I considered freedom to look and feel like. I knew what freedom tasted like from my time living on the IMG campus. But even the Academy had rules. Strict rules by most standards but nothing compared to what it was like living under my parents' roof. My parents were super cool when it came to all things sports. But when it came to leaving the house in the evenings, it wasn't even something I would bring up because there was no point—unless I wanted to hear a speech about all the bad things that happen in the world after dark and during the night. I understood where they were coming from, since their careers were in insurance where everything is based on risk. But when you're a high school kid and all your friends are going to dinner or going to hang out and you know there is no way you can go, you feel suppressed. It also created a deeper feeling inside me that if I did partake in anything that wouldn't be allowed in my house and something did happen it would be 1000 percent my fault because I knew better. Those thoughts stayed with me into adulthood, and

I am working through how not to move through life with so much fear. I trust myself and my decision-making much more now.

College would be freedom on a whole new level. I could leave my dorm at eight and go to CVS, the drugstore across the street. That sounds silly now, but at the time, I was never at liberty to come and go as I pleased. Never. Looking back, I understand why my parents were strict, but I sometimes wished they would have bent the rules around some things because I was such a good kid and listened to them ninety-eight percent of the time.

I had a countdown clock on my Myspace page, ticking away the days until I turned eighteen and got to move out of my parents' home and be on my own. Maybe this is why it was so hard for me to accept financial help from them even when I needed it because I knew taking any money or support would come with the control I was trying to remove from myself ASAP. More on this later.

Mom and Dad took me to Target and Walmart for all the items I'd need in my new dorm: a small fridge, a microwave, and other household items. A shower caddy and slippers and a door organizer for the bathroom.

The University of Miami had two predominantly athlete dorms, which were built in 1965. All the freshman and sophomore scholarship athletes stayed in either Pearson or Mahoney dorms. The floors in those dorms weren't separated by gender. There were normal (non-athlete) students sprinkled in there also, but you didn't usually see freshmen in these dorms. If you were a non-athlete, you stayed in Stanford Residential, which had two huge towers named Walsh and Rosborough. The interesting thing about Stanford was that each floor was either an all-girl floor or an all-boy floor. They didn't regulate boys not going to girls' floors or vice versa, but I think the rules stated that students had to be on their own floor at night. Each floor had communal bathrooms.

My best friend, Shelly, actually stayed in Stanford, so I got a glimpse of normal college life whenever I went to her dorm to hang out with her for the day. Only freshmen stayed in these dorms. I think it may have been strongly suggested that if you were a fresh-man, you should live on campus, and then after that most students moved into their own apartments with roommates or stayed in the University Village, or UV. The UV had apartment-style residences for University of Miami students only.

My floor probably had forty different dorm rooms, and I hap-pened to luck out and get my own room. My parents dropped me off at my new home: a single room on the fourth floor, the top floor. I had the room to myself, no roommates, which was odd. As a single child, I enjoyed having my own place to decorate and live in with no one else around. I knew I'd make friends quickly—I always did. I did find it a bit odd that I didn't get to have that traditional college experience where you have to navigate living with a roommate. I suppose since I had already gone through that at IMG, I was seasoned enough when it came to sharing.

I looked around for other tennis players and discovered that none of them lived on campus. The sophomores, juniors, and seniors lived off campus, most with their spouses, which to me seemed wild back then. I was the only female freshman tennis player on the team, and the only Black American tennis player. All the other girls on the tennis team were from other countries. I wondered, *Why aren't there other American tennis players on the team?*

One reason I picked the University of Miami was because I knew another girl who attended the school, Julia Cohen. She was a couple of years older than me, but I often saw her at the Grand Slams, and I knew she was a great player. Julia was an excellent junior player, reaching a career high of number four in the world. She encouraged me to go to the University of Miami too. Unfortunately, once I was accepted, I found out Julia was leaving. We wouldn't be playing on the team together. I was sad about this, but I had to keep it moving. I couldn't spend too much time thinking about why she left or what could have caused her to no longer be on that team. It should have been a red flag. I pushed the question aside. I was too excited to actually be on my own.

My room was small, with a bathroom and a twin bed, but it was big enough for me. At the Academy, I had roommates. This was the first time I'd be on my own in my own little place. My own bathroom. No bunk beds. No one telling me when to come and go. Heaven. I set to making the room my own right away, tearing pages from fashion magazines and taping them to one wall.

GETTING TO KNOW THE CAMPUS AND STUDENTS

After settling into my new place, I wandered the campus to see who else was around. Athletes could move in before the other students, so for that first week, all I saw were football and basketball players. They had all been there since the summer; since they competed in sports that were in the fall, they already had to be on campus. They looked and acted differently from the students I knew at the Academy. I'd never seen so many Black people together in one place. They looked much older than the kids at the Academy, probably because they were grown men.

The Mahoney and Pearson dorms housed mostly football players. I'd never seen football players in real life because IMG didn't have a football program when I was there. They were huge. Making eye contact with these men was different from when I met new people at the Academy. Some wouldn't smile or say hi. They would just glare at you until you looked away. Others were super friendly and flirtatious, which left me confused on how to respond.

Normal students began moving in. That was an eye-opener. IMG students were all athletes, focused on health, fitness, and being the best in the world. The normal University of Miami students partook in things we could never do at IMG, like smoking cigarettes and taking a lot of prescription drugs.

Many of the non-athletes vaped. I hadn't been around any kind of smoking my entire life. I watched kids flock to the smoking areas of the campus and release these massive plumes of smoke from their vapes. They thought they looked cool, but I was thinking, *Why are you killing yourself slowly?* As I got older and formed my thoughts differently, I learned not to dislike someone just because they did things that I wouldn't do. Not everyone is going to be like me or think like me, and that's okay. I don't focus on those differences, and I keep my opinions to myself.

The University of Miami was gorgeous, like a vacation resort. A massive lake and water fountain in the middle of the campus were surrounded by manicured lawns and greenery. The pool was enormous to accommodate the swimming and diving teams. Students in bathing suits lay out on towels and lawn chairs, tanning in the Florida sun. Compared to larger public schools, the university, a private college, had only a couple thousand freshmen. The close community made it feel more like IMG. The smaller campus meant I could get from class to the tennis courts quickly on my bike.

Freshmen weren't allowed to have cars at the university back then. The campus was small, and parking was limited and very expensive, so I didn't mind that my Volkswagen Beetle stayed at my parents' home. I was on scholarship at a very expensive private school and didn't want to take on unnecessary expenses for myself or my parents. Keep in mind this was way before Uber existed.

I walked and biked everywhere. To leave campus, I took a yellow taxi. Sometimes I went in a friend's car. That was my first exposure to bad driving habits. Some of my friends "knee-drove." While their hands were busy texting on their phones, they used their knees to steer. That terrified me. It was so unsafe! If I got in a car with a knee-driver, I never got in their car a second time, or I would suggest that I drive so I could at least control the situation. Most of the time I became the DD, or designated driver, of my friends because I wanted to ensure we got places safely. A few times, I got into a car and someone pulled out a joint or told me they had weed on them. I'd be so freaked out I'd start hyperventilating.

"What's wrong with you?" they'd ask.

"Nothing," I'd say, "but I have to get out of the car right now."

I wasn't at IMG, so I didn't have to worry about the "in the presence of" rule that could expel me. My dad wasn't in the car with me. Still, I had to take responsibility for myself and make good choices. Getting out of a car in the middle of Miami wasn't a simple decision. There was no Uber, no Lyft. Staying in the car would have been easy. Getting out was hard. But I did it every time.

On three occasions, finding myself in a car with someone who had weed on them, I got out. I couldn't risk getting pulled over and being caught with these people. That rule saved me from some ugly experiences that I didn't have to face. I didn't care if I lost friends in the process. I watched how one bad decision could change someone's whole life trajectory, and it was *not* going to happen to me. Not on my watch.

COLLEGE ACADEMICS: A NEW STRUGGLE

The University of Miami was a tremendous culture shock, and also a massive shock from an academic standpoint. The curriculum was nothing like IMG's. In high school, I had a class and then a whole week, sometimes several weeks, to read the assigned chapter. In college, we covered multiple chapters in a single class session. At IMG, as long as I paid attention in class and skimmed the chapter, I could pass a test and get an A. The University of Miami prided itself on having a tough curriculum and using some of the same academic strategies as Stanford and other top institutions. This did *not* work in my favor because I didn't know how to study or be a star student. My IMG days didn't prepare me for UM's rigorous standards, and not all the professors cared that I was on the tennis team. Some actually treated me worse.

My first semester GPA was two.3. I started out as a psychology major but switched to communications because I couldn't pass my first psychology class. That was embarrassing. I had to face the fact that I was sorely out of practice in reading, learning, and studying. The past eight years had been all about tennis, and I had a lot of catching up to do.

One reason I struggled so much the first semester was the class sizes. I was in a lot of "intro to" courses: Intro to Psychology. Intro to Communications. Classes were held in a large auditorium. I was used to classes of ten or twelve people and a lot of interaction. Suddenly, I was with hundreds of students, listening to lectures. With so many people crammed into a room, I didn't make friends in my classes, so there was no one to talk to about the homework either. I was a little lost.

I was doing well in some classes but poorly in others, bringing my average down. After not studying for so many years, I had forgotten how to do it. Math would be a challenge; I knew that from the start. I didn't expect the courses I usually excelled in to be so hard. Luckily, as a Division I athlete, I had a lot of resources available to me. Knowing I had to step it up or risk losing my scholarship, I committed to spending all my free time in the athletic study hall with tutors.

If I wasn't in class or on the courts, I was in study hall. My tutors were non-athlete University of Miami college students. They were very kind and got a kick out of teaching the athletes, especially if they were paired with a star basketball or football player.

As an athlete, I was assigned an academic advisor who made sure I took all the right courses and kept my grades up. The advisors were very important, and I still remember working with Chris. He knew all the professors and which ones were nicer to athletes or more forgiving with them missing class for tournaments. That made a big difference. With all this support, you'd think the student athletes would all do well. However, not all the players took getting an education seriously. I'd see them in study hall goofing off, on their phones, and being disrespectful. Their tutors would try to engage them in the work, but the situation was awkward, and I felt sorry for them. Imagine getting a free ride to a great college and not being grateful to the people helping you get an education. I realized that not all athletes were interested in academics. For them, playing sports was all that mattered. "Keeping it one hundred" getting to the league was all they cared about.

Some professors had a reputation for being tougher on athletes. Others were more forgiving, or they were unbiased and treated all students the same. If you had to travel for a game and miss a test, an accommodating professor could mean the difference between passing and failing a class. A good advisor ensured you didn't end up in a classroom with a professor who made you choose between your sport and an education.

My second semester GPA was much better; I think I had a three.1 GPA, so I could breathe easier. I wanted an education. I enjoyed learning. I wanted to keep playing tennis too. I hated not getting good grades, and keeping them up was even more important since my eligibility to play on the tennis team relied partly on my academic performance. After raising my GPA, I learned that my classroom struggles weren't due to a lack of intelligence; I just hadn't learned to be a good student yet. That first semester was the training I needed to do well academically in college, and my grades continued to improve.

STAYING OUT OF TROUBLE

I didn't go to parties during my freshman year. No house parties or frat parties. I didn't drink in the dorms, either, mostly because I was underage and scared of getting caught drinking. When a friend of a friend made me a fake ID, I started going to nightclubs. This, for me, was a huge risk, but I was willing to do it because I wanted to have fun. I was eighteen, and I wanted to be able to get into the good clubs that you had to be twenty-one to enter. I just wanted to dance with my friends and have a good time. Even in that environment, I only allowed myself two drinks. That worked out perfectly for me. I never drank outside of a nightclub, and I would only go to the club on some Saturdays. I never wanted to be out of control of my mind or body, so two alcoholic beverages was my limit. There had been a time when I drank three cocktails, and even though nothing bad happened, I felt like it could have. Like, I could have lost my keys, my phone, or my wallet. My father had instilled a good habit in me:

"When you get up to leave a place, always check for your wallet, keys, and phone." I could see forgetting that habit with one too many drinks, so I didn't let it happen. I also saw what happened to the girls who drank too much. They had no control of themselves, and they wouldn't remember their nights. I refused to experience this because it just seemed like a surefire way to get attacked.

I didn't take drugs either. Cocaine and molly seemed to be popular during that time, but I never witnessed anyone doing them. I think they snuck away into bathrooms for that. Also, the people I knew didn't expose me to the stuff they were doing because they knew I was a rule-follower. So I was saved from having to watch people do drugs in front of me, and I'm not mad at that. Drug culture is so normalized today, and I still carry a big stigma toward it because of my upbringing. I say, "Do you, but I'll be over there not doing it."

The University of Miami was known as the Ivy League of the South, on par with prestigious schools like Stanford. I don't know whether that was true, but the curriculum was tough, and they graded on a bell curve. They didn't accept mediocrity, and if you got a C, per the bell curve, you might get an F. I was familiar with this mentality because IMG didn't allow you to be average in sports, either, although their academic standards wouldn't improve until years later.

As much as I cared about my grades, the "regular students"—the non-athletes—placed a lot more importance on academics than I did. When college finals approached, they felt like test scores were a life-or-death situation, as if the world would end if they didn't pass a class. That was the first time I saw non-sports students put as much pressure on themselves as I put on myself for tennis.

At school, a lot of students took Adderall. They called it addy. I'd hear kids in class, at the library, and around campus asking, "You need an addy?" and "You got any addy? I've gotta cram for this test." They were like fiends needing a fix because their mommies and daddies expected them to get straight A's.

My understanding back then was that Adderall was a performance-enhancing drug to help students study. I didn't even realize it was for people with ADHD, a condition that wasn't talked about as much back then. I just knew when the white normal students took it, they stayed up for hours, completely focused on their schoolwork, often without eating. Unlike other drugs I saw them sell, they didn't take Adderall to get high but to maintain their grades and pass their exams, especially during finals weeks. You would see students who looked like zombies because they had been up all night studying on Adderall.

COACH CAROLINE

All my coaches before college were good, and some were great. I'd had only one woman coach before, Margie at IMG. At the time, almost all tennis coaches were men, even at the college level. I wondered what it would be like to play for Coach Caroline. She was so friendly when I visited the campus, before I signed the contract to play tennis for the university.

As a freshman, I was expected to be at the courts early to pull out the balls and set up the courts for the other girls. If I wasn't early enough, I had to run sprints while the other girls watched. I don't think the coach counted on my being accustomed to living under rigid rules. Being at IMG was a primer for college, and I knew how to prepare for anything and be on time.

No matter how early I was or how well I played, Coach Caroline was determined to make my life harder, almost as if she were hazing the new recruit. I was used to tough coaches, but this was a whole new level of meanness. Keep in mind that I was the only freshman on the team. The rest of the girls were from other countries like Germany, France, Spain, Austria, and New Zealand. There I was, the sole freshman from the USA navigating this new college experience alone.

I soon learned Coach Caroline enjoyed making all the players uncomfortable. One of her favorite punishments was forcing us to hold a twenty-five-pound gym plate over our heads while doing wall sits. With no weight at all, wall sits can be hard. With weights, they're brutal. We did plank, too. She would make the girls hold their positions but not let them know how long they had to hold them. So we never knew if we were going to be in pain for one minute or five minutes. That was mentally torturous. I could handle a lot of pain if I knew how long I had to endure it, but not knowing made her punishments much more difficult. Once, a girl holding a plate over her head fell down. The plate hit her on the head and knocked her out. We all wanted to stop to check on her, but Coach Caroline made us stay put.

"Nobody get off the wall," she bellowed. "Hold your positions."

There were other instances where girls were injured during these sessions. One girl suffered permanent internal damage. The coach pitted us against each other too. She created a hierarchy in the team, reserving her kindness for the seniors, as if it were a reward given to those students who survived four years of her abuse. Being the only freshman, I got it the worst. This didn't make sense to me. We were a team. We had to work together to win. Creating internal drama pushed us apart.

MAKING FRIENDS

My friendships got better over time. Amanda and Bianca were roommates, and two of just three Black women in the university's engineering school. Along with another friend from IMG, Moniquee, they introduced me to Black culture. Through them I learned so much more about what was really happening on campus. These girls came to my tennis matches, even though they weren't really into sports. Having that support felt good. I enjoyed hanging out with these girls. I also hung out with a friend from high school, Shelly.

Shelly wasn't from IMG or even a tennis player; I'd met her through a mutual friend of ours, Jovana, and we'd clicked. We were born one day apart; we were both Aries, and we were both students at the University of Miami. Shelly was in AP classes in high school and was on an academic scholarship at the university. She was also

my connection to the non-athletic world, which was a lot different
from the world I lived in. She told me about rush week and getting
into a white sorority. I think I actually went with her and watched
as she walked around and interviewed with all the sororities. This
was very interesting to me because I had never been exposed to this
before. The university had Black sororities, but I wasn't involved in
them. Listening to Shelly, the selection process sounded judgmental
and superficial. Getting into her chosen sorority was important to
Shelly, and I couldn't understand why. My parents had taught me to
steer clear of groups like that.

They'd say, "You don't have to go through all that to have friends.
You're an athlete. People are going to want to hang out with you."

I didn't know if that was true, but since I seemed to have no problem making friends, maybe they were right. What my parents didn't
realize or care about was that a lot of students want to join these
sororities and fraternities because of the networking and connections that come from them after college. I could see why an employer
would be more likely to give a role to their line brother or sister than
someone else even if that other person may be better or more qualified. After getting my fair share of smacks in the face by corporate
America, I can see why parents and students put so much pressure on
being a part of these groups. Most of my college friends were in the
Alpha Kappa Alpha sorority, which is known for wearing pink and
green. These girls were fierce and highly coveted on campus. While
they were in the probate process, being evaluated for acceptance,
they ignored me for a while. They stopped speaking to me and didn't
invite me to do anything with them. I guess there was some kind of
rule about interacting with people outside the sorority. After their
reveal, where they found out whether they were in or out, that all
changed and they started talking to me again. As an outsider who was
friends with probably seven of the thirteen girls in their line, I didn't
understand what was happening, and they weren't able to disclose
anything that was happening inside. I didn't let that bother me or
impact me too much. I, too, was busy and had things I needed to do

all the time with the tennis team. So I just focused on making sure I had my studies together and being a good friend whenever they were able to hang out with me. I'm the opposite of a codependent person, so going to the cafeteria by myself to eat lunch or dinner was normal for me. I would see someone there who I knew, or even if I didn't, I would just make a new friend.

I wasn't jealous of not being in a sorority. I was relieved that I didn't have to go through what they did. I might have missed a lot of sorority parties, but I was better off without the drinking anyway. I didn't want to get drunk, and I had to stay fit and get plenty of rest to play tennis. Their parties were intense and always controlled by the male fraternities.

THE GUY IN THE WHITE BENTLEY

I didn't date much in college. It wasn't like I was or wasn't seeking men, but sometimes they showed up in my life. I would have loved to have had a serious boyfriend like some of my friends had. It just wasn't in the cards for me. Like that day at the mall. The Dadeland Mall is a bougie retail center in Miami where you can find the latest designer fashions and trends. Back then they had even more options like the department stores Nordstrom and Saks. There were valets to park your cars for the people who didn't want to self-park. Shelly and I were checking out some jeans in the True Religion store when I noticed a guy looking at me. Like, *really* looking. He was super tall and maybe in his late thirties or early forties. Not a guy I'd usually pay attention to, but he was hard to miss because of his height. He was well over six feet tall, probably close to six seven, and he was staring at me.

I didn't think much of it. I was a tall girl, and sometimes people just stared at me. I was used to knowing when someone was a basketball player from IMG. I regularly saw people six five and taller, and my high school friend Moniquee was taller than this. Outside, after we finished shopping, Shelly and I slipped into a taxi for the ride back to campus. This was before the luxury of Uber or Lyft. Can you imagine taking a yellow taxi from your dorm room to the mall? The valet man sprinted toward the cab and knocked on the window. I rolled down my window, surprised.

"Wait, ma'am. Don't leave yet," he said. "See that guy in the white Bentley? He wants your phone number."

"What?" I asked.

The valet said his name, and I didn't recognize it. Neither did my friend. The way the guy said it sounded like we should, though. Now I am not in the habit of giving out my number to strangers. However, I was intrigued. Who was this guy anyway? I scrawled my number on a piece of paper—probably the receipt from my bag—and handed it to the valet.

The minute the taxi drove off, Shelly and I googled the guy's name.

"Hmmm...looks like he's a pretty famous basketball player," said Shelly.

I was seeing the same thing. "Penny Hardaway. Born in 1971." So he was a lot older than me. "Looks like he played for the Orlando Magic. Before that the Knicks. He was a pretty big deal."

Shelly and I kind of laughed it off. What did this guy want with me? I wasn't really interested in dating anyone that much older, but I was curious. What was he like anyway? What would it be like to go out with him? Keep in mind any guy our age was not doing what he just did. They were too busy thinking they were too cool to ask a girl out. It's funny; in my whole life I have probably only been asked out on a date maybe five or six times, which is pretty pathetic compared to the generation before me where this would have been the main way people would have gone on dates. Even with social media back then, since Instagram was just beginning (plus Messenger, Snapchat, Facebook, etc.), guys always used the path of least resistance, which was less in person and more virtual. So Penny doing what he did was exciting and different for me.

A couple of days later, I got a text. Would I be up for dinner with him?

I didn't know how to respond, but Shelly, who was always up for an adventure, convinced me.

"Oh my gosh, you should definitely go! Think of where he would take you."

That convertible Bentley was the most expensive, luxurious car I'd ever been in. My parents always did well, but I had always been in a nice Mercedes or a BMW; they didn't explore the fringe luxury vehicles like Range Rover, Bentley, Rolls-Royce, and Ferrari. That was another level. Penny was polite and charming. He seemed surprised when I told him I was in college, and even more surprised when I said I was a freshman. He didn't say it out loud, but I could tell by his expression that he thought I was much older. I could almost see him doing the math in his head, thinking, *This is not going to work*.

We had a nice dinner with good conversation. He was complimentary of me and my maturity and how my mindset was much different than most women he had talked to. After the date, he dropped me off at the common area outside the dorms, a popular spot where students congregated to eat and socialize. I could feel the eyes on me as I slid out of the car, and I'm sure plenty of people were thinking the same thing: *Who is this tall girl, and what is she doing with this big dude in a Bentley coupe?* I still remember football players sitting outside the dorms looking at me as I walked past them to get to my room. We didn't see this type of thing happen on campus, so it was strange for sure.

I kept a low profile about the whole thing. I didn't want or need the extra attention, and I knew from the start the date wouldn't turn into a long-term situation. Realizing the age difference was too great, and we were in completely different phases of our lives to pursue anything serious, we didn't take it any further.

BAD NEWS

Somehow, I survived my freshman year on the tennis team. I also found out why I was the only American player. Coach Caroline had a terrible reputation, and no one in the States wanted to play for her. She recruited girls from outside the US. I wondered how that fact had slipped past Scott, the guy who'd facilitated my college recruitment, and my parents.

Attracting girls to the American tennis team wasn't hard because it came with a full ride. Thanks to Title IX, the university was mandated to provide an equal number of full scholarships to women as to men. So if they gave away one hundred scholarships for men's football, basketball, and other sports, they had to give out one hundred scholarships to women athletes. Girls from other countries who weren't ready to go pro could play Division I sports and get a free education. My tennis team comprised mostly girls from Europe and South America.

After somehow surviving one year, I returned to Miami to get ready for my sophomore year. In that first year as a team, we accomplished a lot. We lost in the finals of the ACC tournament, which was our conference championship. We also lost in the quarterfinals or Elite eight of the NCAA college championships to UCLA, Caroline's alma mater. I got a glimpse of what it was like to compete against the highest level of collegiate athletics. When we were playing against the top schools back then, I saw my fellow girls in Percy's group, the ones who also chose to go to college. I saw Mallory and Mary when we played against Duke. They ended up winning the whole NCAA tournament that year. I saw Carling Jr when we played UCLA, and they beat us in the tournament. After getting back on campus, I knew my sophomore year was going to be tough. I was not excited about coming back because I had just played a summer of pro tournaments. I knew now what to expect with Caroline, and I'd somehow survived her crazy abuse for a year. There were three new freshman girls joining our team, including Kayla, my friend from junior tennis who I grew up with, and Brittany Dubins, another girl from junior tennis who I competed against for years in the twelves and fourteens in Florida tournaments. I played more against her sister Taylor, who was closer to my age, but I knew of the other Dubins sisters as well. And I was happy that two Americans were joining the team. Not that I didn't like being with the other girls. I just wanted to be able to relate stronger to them. Brittany had somehow broken her wrist, I think due to a fall, and her arm was in a cast. She couldn't play tennis, so since she wasn't able to hit with us, Coach Caroline just had her doing random fitness activities. Brittany was vegetarian, so her diet always became a topic of conversation with the coach. She would make comments to the other girls and find any reason to put her down. Coach Caroline couldn't resist embarrassing her in front of the team.

"Brittany, should you really be eating that Power Bar?"

"Brittany, do you really need to be eating that pasta?"

Some girls laughed at the comments. Most of us were sickened by them, especially Kayla and me. We couldn't stand this behavior because it was bullying at its finest.

The worst episode was when Coach Caroline made us run four hundreds around the track. Brittany, still in a full forearm and bicep cast, couldn't run quickly enough to make the coach's "cutoff time." I still have a vivid image in my head. Her cast went almost all the way to her shoulder blade, and she was basically running with one arm. Every time she missed the time, we had to keep running. The tennis team ran dozens of four hundreds around that track. Some girls started yelling at Brittany, as if it were her fault they were being punished. Eventually, girls started crying and throwing up. I executed the run and made the time the first fourteen or fifteen times we ran the four hundreds. After that, not only Brittany but some of us missed the time too. I left like I was dying. Fed up and furious, I walked off the track. I knew from that moment I needed to get off this team and away from this toxic coach.

I thought about the situation. This was not the life I wanted, but what other choice did I have? Quitting the team wasn't a viable option. Tennis was my life. I walked around for a while, then came back to practice.

This was not the coaching I was used to. The harshest words from my IMG coaches were like praise compared to the behavior I witnessed at the University of Miami.

Was it abusive? At the time, I wasn't sure. Looking back, I believe her treatment of the team was an abuse of power. Today, I wouldn't tolerate that treatment from a coach or anyone else. Coach Caroline's actions and behavior should have been investigated. She was a sociology nerd, so she loved seeing how she could manipulate people to do what she wanted them to do or create story lines between the players and create unnecessary drama. This is already a tough time in a young adult's life, being eighteen to twenty years old. You are an adult, but you still need help and guidance. She abused this immensely and broke you down without building you back up. As you can tell, I have no respect or sympathy for this woman, but I can only respect who I became as a result of dealing with her crazy ass. If I had been violent, she would have caught hands from me, but I chose a more practical, satisfying approach I have planned for my future, when I will donate some money to the Miami tennis program and maybe get them to rename the tennis facility after me. Every day she can look up and see my name and remember how rude and nasty she was to me and many other girls just like me. There is a difference between being a tough coach and being a nasty person.

I didn't mention Coach Caroline's behavior to my parents at the time. From a young age, I'd been taught not to complain or make excuses. I couldn't vent to them about anything. If I had a problem, my dad's first question would be, "What did you do?" as in, "What did *you* do that caused this to happen? How did *you* create this problem?" So I learned to keep my problems—including the coach's abuse—to myself.

Walking out of practice just made my problems worse. Now I had a target on my back.

MIAMI NIGHTLIFE

I couldn't bring my car to college my freshman year. In my sophomore year, my first car, a white 2008 Volkswagen Beetle, came with me. I was often called upon to drive my friends to places, including the nightclubs.

Going to Miami clubs was a whole new world for me. I met promoters who could get me and my girlfriends into all the bougie hip-hop places. I steered clear of the rougher nightclubs, where guys were too aggressive and sometimes violent. The bigger, roomier clubs appealed to me, where I had space to dance without bumping into people and feeling claustrophobic.

We had to arrive early because the promoters wanted to fill the place with pretty girls before everyone else showed up. My friends and I would get a table and a bottle (the table always came with vodka), and we'd dance to rap and hip-hop music all night—or however long the party lasted.

During the offseason, that was my typical Saturday night. I usually had tennis practice on Saturday mornings, so I avoided going out on Friday nights. The one time I did, I regretted it. I wasn't a big drinker, usually having a couple of vodka and cranberry or vodka and pineapple cocktails, so I was never hungover. I needed sleep to play well, though, so going out the night before tennis was off the table. When I was playing in tournaments, I didn't go out at all.

My friends and I were very safety-conscious, so my self-imposed two-drink maximum helped. Occasionally, like on my birthday, when I might celebrate more than usual, I'd ask someone else to drive. I looked out not only for my own safety, but for everyone else's. Being under twenty-one, I couldn't risk any of us getting in trouble because I'd get dragged into it. The repercussions of my actions were always on my mind: *What if I get caught drinking? Could I lose my scholarship? Get kicked out of school?* I didn't know, and I didn't want to find out.

Looking back, it's a miracle I didn't go absolutely wild in college. I knew kids who, like me, were raised in super strict families, and when they got their first taste of freedom, they rebelled, getting into all sorts of trouble. My behavior didn't waver, in part because I didn't want to disappoint my parents, but also because I didn't want to ruin my life. I had seen the consequences of bad decisions—promising young athletes losing scholarships, getting kicked out of school, and forfeiting sports careers. I didn't spend a decade and a half working toward something to turn around and risk it all for a night on the town.

I stayed away from the parties and set my focus on the amazing clubs that Miami had to offer on Saturdays. I would go to Dream, Cameo, or Play. Those were the three nightclubs that we would frequent back in college. Back then, promoters controlled everything, and I was lucky to meet a promoter who went by the name Blu. He had blue eyes and that was why they called him Blu. After I met him, he let me know that as long as I came by the club by 11:30 with my girls, we could get in free and be at his table. So I became the plug for going out to my friends. This caused a lot of girls to want to be around us just for my club connections. I learned later these superficial relationships were not helpful. Also keep in mind that there were hundreds of clubs in Miami at the time. The club scene was rampant, and as young adults trying to find ourselves, my friends and I really enjoyed those three clubs I mentioned because they had what we needed to feel safe and secure: (one) good music, hip-hop, but in an upscale environment; (two) our own table or section, which was important so we could dance and be free and not be claustrophobic and have men try to dance with us or talk to us, like a bubble we could have fun in and feel safe; and (three) a guaranteed way in for free.

Being women who were cute, we never paid for anything, which was the norm, but we had to follow the rules by getting there early, filling out the section, and making it look good for the male athletes or entertainers who would be the ones actually spending money on sections and bottles. One lady I met through this process ran the 400 Club, a promotions company. She threw the best parties. Her name was Jess, and back then it was Simply Jess. She was a huge connection, and she always made sure I was taken care of at the club. She really was one of the only women out there doing huge numbers for her parties, and all the celebrities wanted to go out to her events. She's since left that environment and become a talented artist with exhibits being showcased at Art Basel. We stay in touch through social media and cheer each other on. She's a fellow Aries, and I know that whatever she does she's going to be the best at. She had that same drive and focus that I have.

MY SOPHOMORE YEAR

I was thrilled to learn that one of my friends was coming to the University of Miami. I knew Kayla from junior tennis. She knew I was playing tennis at the university, so she applied and was accepted. We got to play together my sophomore year.

Summer break gave me a reprieve from Coach Caroline. Entering my sophomore year, I had several more months of pro tournaments to look forward to. I was still working with Ales and excited to get away and compete. I had to get through college team practices with Coach Caroline and was hoping to find a solution for surviving her cruelty by the springtime, when team tournaments started. Just as I'd done the previous year, I let her know when my first pro tournament was coming up.

"No. I need you to play in this college tournament that weekend," she said.

Wait a minute, I thought. *The main reason I chose the University of Miami was because the college agreed to let me play pro during the fall.* That was how we'd operated throughout my freshman year. What was going on?

She wouldn't change her mind. It was like she'd pulled a bait and switch on me. Like she was sabotaging my professional career.

Scott Tribley worked for IMG as the liaison between student athletes and colleges and universities. He helped students through the college recruiting process, which included SAT/ACT prep. My parents and I had trusted him to handle the negotiations between me and the university. He'd tell me what I needed to do to accept the scholarship—like get my SAT scores up. Scott knew that playing pro while in college was the main reason I chose the University of Miami. Well, come to find out, the stipulation allowing me to play pro outside of the spring season was left out of the contract. Even though my parents and I made it clear that that was a major deciding factor in choosing the University of Miami, and even though Scott discussed the topic with the coach and she agreed to that deal, Scott didn't include it in the agreement. Any promises Coach Caroline made to us that weren't in the contract were meaningless. That was a lesson I learned the hard way and never forgot: if it matters, get it in writing.

THE INJURIES BEGIN

My injuries began at the University of Miami. Since tennis isn't a huge revenue-producing sport for colleges, players don't get the best support. We should have had a tennis-specific strength and conditioning coach. Instead, one of the football team's assistant training coaches was assigned to the women's tennis and soccer teams. Coach Barry had played Division I college football, and no doubt he understood how football players should train for their sport. His workouts made no sense for tennis. They made no sense for the players' bodies, skills, or needs. Coach Barry pushed us to max out on large muscle group exercises like squats and bench presses, cleans, and many Olympic-style exercises. That method is great for building mass, but tennis relies on fitness, agility, fast-twitch muscles, and quick response times. Getting bigger didn't make sense for the team and could slow us down and even hurt us.

No matter what we did, Coach Barry wanted us to add more weight. The injuries started right away. Girls complained about shoulder pain, hip pain, tweaked muscles and joints. For the first time in my life, my knees started hurting.

What began as an occasional sharp pain grew to a constant ache in both knees. I started taking over-the-counter painkillers. Before practice or a game, I needed eight to ten Advil. When that stopped working, I got cortisone shots in both knees. This was all new to me.

Up until then, I had been in pristine health. No pain outside of the typical muscle soreness after a long workout or game, but no injuries or lingering aches.

In hindsight, I wish I had spoken up and refused to do the workouts. The damage they were causing was obvious, but I had always trusted my coaches. That was probably the first time I realized that just because someone—including a coach—was in a position of authority didn't mean they knew what was best for me. I wish I had had the good sense to realize that I could walk away.

I don't believe that the coach didn't have my best interests at heart; he simply didn't know how to train tennis players. He just assumed that whatever he was doing for football would work for tennis. If I had gone to my parents, I don't think they would have helped. Like me, they trusted the "experts"—the coaches. The minute the alarms started going off in my head telling me the workouts were wrong for me, I should have walked away and refused to do them. I should have asked my parents to get a second coach's opinion on the training and a second doctor's opinion on the treatment. They would have told us what we needed to hear from "the experts"—to stop doing what I was doing before my knees were damaged permanently.

Unfortunately, I didn't have the presence of mind to seek others' perspectives on the situation. My parents weren't coming to my practices like they did at IMG but only showing up for games. They weren't aware of what I was going through.

I complained to the coaches. They told me my pain was normal. It didn't feel normal to me. I was hurting, and my pain wasn't being validated but pushed aside, as if what I knew to be true wasn't.

DATING

My parents prepared me for a lot of things. They never talked to me about men. Maybe they wanted to pretend that part of my life didn't exist. Whatever they were thinking, I went to college totally unprepared for how a lot of men at that age see women. As the new tennis player at the University of Miami, I was like raw meat thrown into the lion's den.

I also didn't realize how insecure young men are, and how they stroke their egos by pretending to like multiple women at the same time, leading them on to develop a sort of "following" of admirers. Pathetic.

My rude awakening began when the quarterback of the University of Miami's football team started texting me. The Hurricanes were doing well, so he was a big deal. "Devon" seemed genuinely interested in me, and for weeks, we texted back and forth. His messages felt like the beginning of a romantic relationship, and I was excited to spend time with him.

Until he ghosted me. I didn't know what was going on. Had I said something? Done something? A few days later, I was standing in line at the cafeteria when I overheard a couple of pretty white girls mention his name.

"I don't know why Devon just stopped talking to me."

That got my attention.

"Wait," I interrupted. "Are you dating him?"

She was. Or thought she was. Just like I thought I was, or at least headed in that direction. That was a huge wake-up call: young men, especially star football players, didn't see women as people but as conquests. I didn't regret the texting; in fact, I was happy to find out what was going on before I went any further with that kind of "relationship." So thanks, Devon, for teaching me who *not* to date. The girl in line at the cafeteria became a friend of mine, us bonding over that lesson.

We soon learned that male college athletes sent the same text messages to dozens of women at once, seeing which ones would bite. That made me question my dating habits. I'd been out with other athletes. Were they texting and dating other women? I didn't wait to find out. I stopped dating completely for a while. I was just over it all. This wasn't like IMG, where there was more mutual respect for women and female athletes. At IMG, the guys saw the way we trained and competed, and they respected that, which altered the way they would speak and engage with us. At college, many of these football and basketball players couldn't care less what you did on or off the court or field. They just saw you as a female they were trying to conquer and add to their list of attractive women they could brag to their teammates about. This was an adjustment for me for sure. I came in expecting the environment to mirror what I had at IMG, being friends with all the athletes from all the sports. It just felt different. It could also have been because we were all college age and hormones were rampant. Nobody wanted to be friends anymore. They all just wanted to hook up. I realized this was not going to work for me.

MY FIRST BOYFRIEND

"Peter" was my first real college boyfriend. I met him toward the end of my sophomore year. A postgraduate, he was studying for his master's in physical therapy. Peter was also a volunteer coach for the women's basketball team. He was mixed like me, but he had the most beautiful green eyes. Ever since I was little, I've always loved a man with pretty eyes. I mean, who doesn't love that? He wasn't super tall like I was used to, probably my exact height or maybe half an inch taller than me. Keep in mind at this point, at nineteen turning twenty, I was a solid five eleven. He was super nice and very smart, and we got along well. Until we didn't.

I had a lot of male friends in college, mostly the athletes. One night, I went to a house party without Peter; it was for an NBA finals game or something. A football player had invited a bunch of us over from all different sports. There were probably thirty people in his small apartment gathered around the huge flat-screen TV. One of Peter's friends saw me walking into the football player's apartment and told Peter about it. He freaked out, telling me I couldn't hang out with other men, that it was disrespectful, and I was out of line. *What the heck?* I thought. *No male friends?* We had a huge fight and stopped talking for a while, but then I took him back. I was still immature back then, and I didn't understand what was so wrong about what I did. There were other women there, many people. I wasn't alone with another guy, just him and I.

A few weeks later, I was at his apartment. We had finished a meal, and I was helping wash the dishes when he freaked out on me again, telling me I was washing the dishes all wrong: "Why aren't you doing it like this? You need to be scrubbing them this way. Who told you how to wash dishes?"

Okay, so he was super jealous and controlling. I don't know why I gave Peter another chance, but I did. In the back of my mind I knew this didn't feel right to me. And I'm not the most domesticated woman, especially back then. So even if my dishwashing wasn't grade A? It was the tone and the way he said this to me that turned me *off*. It gave me flashbacks of being told what to do by my dad or a coach, and I wanted to escape immediately.

A couple of weeks later, we were at his apartment again, and this time, I brought my friends Amanda and Bianca along to meet him. I was still excited about Peter. Outside of the random outbursts of controlling messaging, he was great, and we had a blast together riding around in his Ford Mustang and going out to eat. Bianca had a stuffed animal with her—a little monkey. She and Peter were talking, getting to know one another, and he picked up the monkey and started playing with it unconsciously. Then he tried to twist its head off. I didn't see it happen, but Bianca told me about it later. "There is something wrong with that guy, Danielle," she said. "You have to stop seeing him." Those red flags! I don't know why we don't see them, or choose to ignore them, but in hindsight, they're so obvious.

I broke it off with Peter. In a public place because I didn't know how he'd react if we were alone and didn't want to find out. I hit him with the line that they say in movies because I didn't know what else to say. I also knew at this time that I would be leaving Miami to go to Tampa, and I knew I didn't want to stay with him for this transition. At this point in my life, I was not willing to give up having guy friends or be in a relationship with so many rules. I felt like he was taking away my freedom, and that couldn't happen. So I said, "It's not you. It's me. I think we need to see other people. I wish you the best, and I'll always cheer for you. I have to go now. Bye."

I walked away without a goodbye hug or anything. My adrenaline was pumping, and I didn't look back. He never called or texted me again. It wasn't until a decade went by that he found me on LinkedIn. It's funny how time can change everything. In retrospect I probably exaggerated some of the feelings I had with him out of immaturity and not understanding what it means to be in a serious committed relationship. He was also three years my senior, so he had different expectations. I'm still thankful for the lessons he taught me about myself.

ANOTHER TOUGH DECISION

In college tennis, the top five players play against each other, with the best player from each school playing against the best player from the other school, the second-best playing against one another, and so forth. To win the tournament, three of your players had to win their matches. If you were the third winner on your team, the clincher, you'd get pulled for interviews.

During my freshman and sophomore years at the university, our team was among the top five in the nation. We were expected to win every match against every school we played, and that created a lot of pressure. There could be no bad days. The only time the pressure eased was when we played against the other four schools in the top five.

The NCAA championship is the biggest college tournament of the year. All the schools in the country compete against each other, and a team has to win about seven or eight matches to take the whole thing.

The University of Miami would get within a couple of matches of winning and then lose to the University of Florida or UCLA. Coach Caroline's energy would change toward us before the UCLA games, and I thought it was because the school was ranked higher, but it might have had something to do with the fact that UCLA was her alma mater and she just didn't want to see them lose. I guess I'll never know.

Regardless, I didn't trust her as my coach. The mean-spiritedness she brought to the team and the ruthlessness with which she treated me and the other players were bad for my head. Plus, the training under Coach Barry was causing me more pain and injuries.

I still hadn't told my parents about how the tennis coach treated me or about my ongoing physical pain. They didn't know that Coach Caroline liked to get in my head and make me feel bad about myself. I didn't tell them she made insulting comments about my personal life that were none of her business. That affected my playing as much as the injuries. Looking back, I'm upset that I let her have such an impact on me. She consumed so much of my time, and she truly made it miserable. Outside of my tennis, I loved everything about being a Miami Hurricane. I wore the school colors with pride, and I loved all the songs and traditions. I was starting to do better in school, so I had more confidence in my classes and with my professors.

Desperate to save my mind, body, and tennis career, I went to my dad and told him the environment wasn't conducive to my development as a tennis player. I told him the coach wasn't allowing me to play pro. I didn't tell him about all the other stuff that was going on—only what I knew he cared about most, which was me playing professional tennis.

Dad listened and acted immediately. He reconnected with Scott, our liaison who'd guided me to the University of Miami. This time, my father was clear about two non-negotiables: "Danielle has to play in a warm environment. More importantly, she has to play professionally through the fall and summers."

Several schools were interested, including the University of South Florida. My first reaction was, *Ugh, are you kidding me?* Miami was among the top five in the country. USF was around twenty-five in the rankings.

Then I took a step back and thought about what it could be like going to South Florida. The school really wanted me. They wanted me to play professionally. The campus was in Tampa, closer to my parents' home.

I visited the university and met with the coach. He and I connected immediately. I didn't sense any drama from him, which was exactly what I needed after Coach Caroline. This new coach, Coach Agustín Moreno, was from Mexico. He cared about the girls, the team, and winning.

Back then, a tennis player could notify the NCAA that they were transferring to a different school without telling their coach. I quickly made the transfer official, so when Coach Caroline discovered I was leaving her team, she couldn't do anything about it. I was very lucky to have Scott in my corner to guide me through this process.

Around this time, Kayla also tried to transfer. She was incredibly strong, physically and mentally. While other girls were puking or bleeding after training with Coach Caroline on the court or with Coach Barry on the track or in the weight room, Kayla never cracked. She was intent on staying on the team—until she also started getting injured. She also wanted to play pro but, like me, wasn't allowed. Kayla didn't have someone like Scott to help her out, and she didn't know how to transfer without letting her coach know. When Coach Caroline found out Kayla was looking at other schools, she started talking about her as if she were a poor player. It seemed as if she was out to sabotage Kayla's career too.

I had to complete my season at Miami, which meant three more months playing for Coach Caroline. Once she heard about my transfer, she came down on me even harder. She tried to turn the other girls against me, dissuading them from speaking to me. If they associated with me, she came down on them too. The coach essentially made me the team's punching bag. For those three months, no one on the team could engage with me on or off the courts. I continued playing well, even though I was miserable. It was terrible because if the other girls talked to me, they would catch hell from Coach Caroline. It was the most isolating time of my life, and I knew they couldn't do anything about it. I never was upset at my teammates. I knew they were trying to survive. They came from other countries, and being DI scholarship athletes allowed them to stay in America, where they wanted to learn and eventually get jobs and have careers. Saying goodbye to the coach, the team, and the University of Miami couldn't come soon enough. I was looking forward to a new beginning where nobody knew me. I was starting fresh, starting from scratch, and ready to make a big impact in Tampa, Florida.

9

THE UNIVERSITY OF SOUTH FLORIDA

Despite Coach Caroline's interference, Kayla was able to find a great school to transfer to, the College of William & Mary in Virginia. After her freshman year at UM, she transferred first to William & Mary and then to the University of South Florida for her sophomore year. I was a junior, just a year ahead of Kayla at South Florida. That summer, after leaving Miami, she and I traveled to Portugal to play doubles in three tournaments. My Czech coach, Ales, came with us.

The court was turf with sand, not like anything I'd played on before. We wore spiked shoes for traction, which we usually wore on grass courts. I hadn't practiced on that surface because it's so rare, typically found in India. The sand made the court slippery. As challenging as the court was, Kayla and I won the first doubles tournament. It was 2011, and the prize money was $10,000. That was the first pro tournament I had ever won! I had won matches, but never a tournament. This was a big deal. We felt like we'd finally made it.

My parents weren't there, but they sure heard all about it! I made sure to capture the trophy ceremony. My mom did such an incredible job documenting my journey through pictures and videos. Whenever my parents didn't travel with me, I tried to keep up that level so I could give the pictures to my mom for our albums.

The following week, we played in the second tournament. Kayla and I won the first two rounds. Then she got food poisoning. She wasn't just a little sick but very ill. Part of me was really disappointed because we were playing so well and might have won all three tournaments together. Another part of me wanted my friend to take care of herself, and I understood when she wanted to go home.

I scrambled to find another doubles partner. I was partnered with Mariana Correa, an Ecuadorian player who'd had a stunning junior career. She was at this tournament with her young son, who was running around the courts and somehow had somebody to watch him while we were playing. I could see her eye on him at all times. He couldn't have been much older than five or six years old. I knew at that moment if I was going to be a mom I was going to need serious support, since I could see how challenging it was to manage him all while maintaining the lift of a pro tennis player. She did it alone, which I was very impressed by. Mariana and I made it to the finals of the tournament together. The third tournament didn't go as well, but I left Portugal with a full heart. Nothing could bring me down after my first tournament win.

A FRESH START

The University of South Florida was a clean slate for me. There was no one spreading rumors about me, no one going behind my back to turn people against me. Miami taught me to be more strategic not only in my tennis but in my personal life as well. I decided right away not to date any USF athletes. I'd be selective about the girls I got close to and guard the details of my life. That is the beauty of a clean slate.

I came to the University of South Florida as a junior. Just one girl, Irene, was older than me. Like the University of Miami, except for Kayla, all the girls on the tennis team were from different countries.

For a senior player on a top-twenty-five team, the pressure to perform compared to Miami was like night and day. I started enjoying tennis again—even the training and the drills. For the first time in months, I was happy. I didn't let up, though. I wanted to maintain my level of fitness and performance and continue to improve. Immediately, I was made captain of the team. I pushed myself and the other girls to do better, try harder. Not like what I had just come from—that was unsafe. I just wanted to lift the team up and win more games. This was a chance to flex my leadership skills.

THE PAIN PERSISTS

I was still experiencing severe pain—constant reminders of my time at the University of Miami. The shooting aches in my kneecaps were unbearable without painkillers. Eight to ten Advil and a lot of work to warm up my legs and knees before every game made playing possible, along with knee braces during play to relieve the pressure. The cartilage around the patellas was wearing down, and every time I took a step, the bones crushed against each other. After a game, I had to ice my knees to bring down the swelling. I had never experienced anything like this at IMG.

Here I was, in my prime and playing my best, and the injuries I'd sustained at Miami were haunting me, threatening to derail my career.

Walking hurt. Stairs hurt more. Changes in weather hurt. I couldn't wear heels.

I don't remember the exact moment, but a time came when the pain became so unbearable, I realized something was wrong with me. This wasn't normal aches and pains that my parents and coaches said it was. It wasn't something "all athletes deal with."

An MRI showed a torn meniscus, not in one knee but in both of them. I thought about all those months of being told to "get used to it" and "toughen up," when I knew deep down something was seriously wrong. Finally, I felt validated.

I went to the head athletic trainer at South Florida for advice. He recommended surgery. He said they could shave off part of the meniscus that was torn, and that would ease the pain. In the world of athletic injuries, a meniscus tear is bad but not the worst that can happen. Not like an ACL tear or an Achilles tendon injury. In my world, where I'd never dealt with surgery, rehab, or taking a break from tennis at all, the idea of letting a surgeon cut open my knees was a huge deal. I was sad about it, and my father was even more depressed. I imagined him doing the math in his head: *She'll be out for X weeks for surgery, then healing and physical therapy, then ramping back up to where she was...* I might be off the courts and out of tennis for five months.

The timing couldn't have been worse. In tennis, you're only as good as your previous year's best tournaments. In 2011, as a college sophomore, I had just come off a great year. If I couldn't match it, I'd lose those pro points.

Before my surgery, my father was planning my return to tennis.

The hospital was on the USF campus. The day before surgery, my mom stayed with me at a hotel across the street. I was a nervous wreck, not knowing what to expect. I worried about the anesthesia. I worried about having both knees operated on at the same time. I'd discussed with my parents having them done separately, but that meant a longer recovery time. What if something went wrong? What if I could never play tennis again? Never walk again?

After the surgery, I woke up in a wheelchair and looked down at my knees, wrapped in massive bandages. My dad didn't visit. I don't think he could bear seeing me like that, incapacitated and unable to play tennis. He sent my mother, and she took me back to the hotel, where I rested for a couple of days. I was on pain meds, which blocked up my digestive system. Nothing seemed to work—not my bladder, not my colon. I was miserable. Imagine sitting on the toilet wanting to pee so badly and only a dribble would run down my leg. It was worse for number twos. I couldn't go to the bathroom for a week, even though I wanted to. The pain meds caused so much constipation; it was tortuous.

My mother stayed with me until I went back to school. Eventually, I went from the wheelchair to using a walker. The first week back was bad; I hobbled between classes and physical therapy with that walker. It was embarrassing. At the athletic training center, I looked and felt like an old person. I was in my early twenties and could barely stand up. Once I got off the walker, I felt better about myself, like I had a chance to bounce back. Still, it was extremely embarrassing being so fit and so young but moving around like a elderly person. The same embarrassment of hobbling to classes and being seen by the athletes was tough. They looked at me like *Damn, I hope I don't have to get surgery.* That's the thing with being an athlete. At some point in time ninety percent of athletes experience an injury that requires surgery. For every athlete, the process is terrible because you end up spending more time in the physical therapy room than on the court or field. Practicing or playing requires so much time and prep work to warm up the muscles to get ready, only to immediately, after play or practice, ice everything down and use stim electrode therapy or red-light therapy to help heal the muscles and tendons that were under so much pain. Practice was so painful. Matches were painful. Tournaments were painful. Honestly, I couldn't tell you what hurt more, before surgery or after surgery. Knowing what I know today and with biohacking and stem cell therapy being so much more prevalent, I would have done so many more things before deciding to get cut open. You never feel the same after surgery. I may have had four or five months of pain-free tennis before all the same pains crept back into my life. I could feels the tears forming in the corners of my eyes because it was such a journey to get my fitness and body back after surgery. To then feel all those same paints all over again, I was crushed.

Training consisted of endurance and strength training without pressure on my knees. I used a hyperbaric treadmill so my muscles wouldn't atrophy. My recovery time was estimated at seven to nine weeks. I came back in five. Probably too soon—that was what it felt like. I was also feeling pressure to get back on the court. I had points falling off that I would lose if I didn't start playing right away, despite how ready I felt. I'm sorry, but there is never a time where you feel "ready" when they cut you open and you heal. You never feel like yourself again. Even now, I still hear clicks in my knees when I do a deep squat. I'm sure everything is okay in there, and I'm also thirty pounds lighter than I was when I played professional tennis, but still to this day, I don't feel the same. This is why I'm so vocal when players ask me if they should do surgery. I always tell them to exhaust all avenues before they cut into you.

The next time I saw my father was in Waterloo, Canada. It was my first tournament after surgery. Post-surgery practice had been scary. Playing in that tournament was scarier. I was terrified of bending the wrong way and snapping a bone, tearing a tendon. In my mind, I needed at least another week to heal, but I felt as if the choice wasn't mine. Other people, including my dad, counted on me, and I didn't want to disappoint them. Mentally, that was the toughest time for me as far as my tennis career. I felt so vulnerable and afraid, but I pushed through.

Fear of losing my pro points fueled my premature return too. I hit the court wearing massive knee braces, which didn't look good for me and probably gave my opponent a lot of confidence. Tennis is an aesthetic sport, and if you don't look good, everyone—the players, the crowd—picks up on it. The opponent, seeing the weakness, hits the ball all over the court to make you run around. Between that and holding back for fear of reinjuring myself, I played poorly and lost in the first round.

Slowly, after weeks of training and healing, I finally recovered.

FINDING MY WAY IN RELATIONSHIPS

I took everything I learned at the University of Miami with me to the University of South Florida. Those lessons came in handy for me and other girls. When my friend Ciara, a volleyball player, started as a freshman, I could see the men circling immediately. I told her the real score: "Ciara, you're going to be flattered, getting all this attention from the athletes. The football players, basketball players. Since you're a good girl, a nice girl like me, you won't want to offend them, so you'll be kind. Well, listen: they have one thing and one thing only on their minds, and you do not want to get caught up in their trap. Steer clear. Don't date at all for a while. Just enjoy being a freshman, a college student. Have friends, boys and girls. But don't think every guy who compliments you is actually interested in a relationship—especially if he's an athlete. Stay clear and don't give them any attention. Don't look their way. Don't smile at them. Don't even make eye contact."

That was the advice I needed and never received before heading off to college. It's kind of ironic, considering all the coaching, guidance, and advice I got for my tennis career!

At South Florida, I didn't date college athletes. I had learned my lesson in Miami. Instead, I started dating pro athletes. And I learned a lot in the process.

Other girls waited for guys to talk to them. Not me. I was outgoing and thought reaching out to network with other athletes was the smart thing to do. I didn't realize men weren't used to that. They saw my extroversion as availability and interest, and not in a professional way.

Twitter was a popular social media platform for connecting with people. I commented on a post by "Grant" of the Buccaneers, and he responded. We started a private conversation, realized we were both in Tampa, and met up at—of all places—the local CVS. Yes, the drugstore.

He was a big guy, six foot eight and 340 pounds. We chatted in the parking lot. It was hot out, midsummer. After that, we dated casually—nothing serious. We were both busy with our sports schedules. I traveled a lot for tournaments. He was busy with preseason and then his NFL season.

Grant was nice, but like other athletes I'd known, he didn't value my sport and the effort I put into it as much as his own. Professional men's sports and the players get a lot of attention. Pro athletes' egos get inflated, and sometimes they forget other people work just as hard as they do for sports and other pursuits that are just as important as football or basketball is to them.

Don't get me wrong. I like men with drive. Unfortunately, they don't all want partners with the same drive—as if their girlfriend's passion somehow takes away from their own. Grant asked me to come to his games, but he *never* came to mine. He never showed up to support me or cheer me on as I played and competed around the globe.

Unfortunately, dating athletes trained me to expect the worst from my partners. For a long time, I expected my boyfriends to demand being the center of attention. I expected them to cheat. I figured all men were narcissistic. I got used to being mistreated. They didn't care about me, my sport, or my tournament schedule. They just wanted me to be available to them when they wanted. At their beck and call. And that wasn't possible. I had my own goals, my own career, my own success, and my own money. Which meant the control they tried on me didn't work. It was so easy to pick an unathletic pretty girl who would be their shadow than to date someone like me who was on the road thirty weeks a year, traveling and competing all over the world.

That's not to say all athletes are this way—just that the ones I knew definitely were. I can almost understand how they got that way as young men, having people cheering for them, wanting to date them and be their friends. In truth, I knew women who sought professional players to latch onto, with the goal of getting married, having kids, and never having to work or worry about finances. I was never that girl, never a so-called gold digger or cleat chaser. I was a woman with my own goals and dreams, not somebody's sidekick. Whenever I heard women talk about how they were scheming to meet this or that player—how they planned to get pregnant and essentially trap a guy—I was disgusted. How could they do that to another person? How could they do that to *themselves*? Not me!

TENNIS AND DATING

As a pro tennis player, I found dating difficult. I was always training, traveling, or playing in a tournament. Then there was the overarching attitude among coaches and parents that tennis requires one hundred percent of the player's focus and anything else is a distraction. Having a significant other was frowned upon.

Tennis players struggle with relationships in general because we have to be very self-centered to succeed. I noticed that some tennis players married their coaches, despite the age gap. I believe this happened partly because they felt guilty about spending time with other people. The age difference was even more dramatic among players in other countries, with some girls as young as sixteen marrying coaches old enough to be their dads.

Dating a coach allows a player to have a romantic relationship without sacrificing tennis. The partnership can work well if the player is winning, but if they're losing, things can go badly. When a player's losing, the first person they blame is their coach. I've seen instances where a player dates another player's coach, which is interesting when the tennis players compete against one another on the court.

In tennis, everybody functions as an independent contractor. There is no human resources department to step in and say, "Hey, maybe this relationship isn't appropriate. There's a power dynamic going on and a good possibility that this girl is feeling pressured to comply."

Of course, players can fire their coaches. Some players hire and fire coaches regularly, but coach hopping is costly, and for most players, someone else is picking up the bill. Unless a player is at the highest level in the game, they can't afford to change coaches every time they lose a tournament.

THE PAIN RETURNS

After I recovered from knee surgery, the pain subsided, and I felt better for about eight months. It never went away completely, though. Increasingly, the pain crept back into my knees—not as bad as before, but they hurt. I was devastated. After all that work to recover, I was back where I started, playing in pain.

Another MRI proved I had little meniscus left in either knee, and the patellas were rubbing against other bones. Doctors told me there wasn't much they could do.

I had to learn to live with the pain.

I'd already been playing doubles, but this news clarified that shifting away from singles made sense. I couldn't cover the entire court anymore. Covering half the court meant less pounding on my joints. I would never play as well as I did before the surgery, but I would still play. I wasn't ready to quit.

A COLLEGE GRADUATE

After doing an extra semester to make up for the time I missed due to surgeries, I graduated from the University of South Florida in 2013. That last semester was the first time I felt like a normal student because I wasn't attached to the USF tennis team. At twenty-two years young, I practiced and played in tournaments, but at school, I just went to classes.

My grandmother attended the graduation. I was so proud of myself, and proud to make her and my parents proud. Despite all the obstacles, ups and downs, and pros and cons of college, walking across that stage to accept my diploma was rewarding. My parents and grandmother finished college, and I didn't want to break that tradition. More importantly, graduating was something I did for me. Not to please my parents or coaches but for Danielle.

10

LIFE ON THE ROAD

As a student, explaining to people who didn't play sports that I was a professional tennis player without the money to go with the status was awkward. They didn't understand that I could keep only enough of my winnings to cover my expenses. After graduating, I could keep everything I won. I realized that might not amount to much, especially at first.

A common misconception about professional athletes is that they all make a lot of money. In fact, only those at the highest levels earn substantial cash. I had glimpses of what that looked like when I played in the bigger tournaments. During most of my professional career, I was lucky to earn $5,000 at a tournament—a pittance considering what it cost to get to that point. I had expenses, including rent on an apartment I moved into after college.

My parents still helped me out financially. That wasn't the case for many players on the road. I traveled to tournaments where five or six girls shared a hotel room, with two to a bed. Sometimes, a wealthy tennis fan would offer a room in their home to put up tennis players while they were in town for a tournament. This was called "housing." Girls signed up for housing with members of the local country club, and they'd get free room and board. That might seem like a small thing, but for a girl with no income, a week of hotels and restaurants is extremely expensive. Imagine being on the road for three weeks with tournaments in Louisville, Nashville, and Memphis. Having a generous patron offset those costs could mean the difference between playing and staying home.

I traveled on my own a lot after college. My parents sent me money when I asked for it, but as an adult and a pro, I wanted to be self-sufficient. On the road, I roomed with other girls and tried to get housing. I didn't want to depend on my parents my whole life, but supporting myself through tennis wouldn't happen overnight, if at all.

RIVIERA MAYA, MEXICO

To develop local talent, Mexico held $10,000 tournaments every week throughout the summer in 2013. My parents signed me up for back-to-back tournaments over three weeks, held at the all-inclusive Grand Palladium Resort. This wasn't a place popular with American tourists. It was a little older and catered to people from Latin American countries. The tournament took over the whole place. Surrounded by a jungle-like environment along the beach, the property attracted the native animals, including huge iguanas that could show up on your doorstep. The bugs were enormous, and I did my best to keep them out of the room I shared with another player.

Our room had air-conditioning, but not the kind I was used to. Like many countries I visited for tennis, the standards for appliances weren't on par with the US. Air-conditioning was often a window unit that maybe worked, or maybe didn't. If I had been there on vacation, I probably wouldn't have noticed, but being in a place for three weeks, the inconveniences got to me.

Some people travel and never unpack, taking things from their suitcases as they need them. For me, traveling as much as I did, a sense of home was important. I unpacked everything and fixed up hotel rooms to look like my place.

After living in Florida for years, I thought I could deal with the heat. The Tampa heat was nothing compared to Mexico in the summer. The Mexican heat was wet like a steam room. Sometimes I felt as if I were being baked from the inside out. It was extremely humid. I felt as if I were melting, constantly sweating, soaking through my clothes. I had never experienced such heat. I learned to pack four changes of clothes, half a dozen pairs of socks, and three pairs of tennis shoes for every match. Girls' feet would perspire so much, they'd move across the court and slip out of their shoes! The court was visibly wet in places from dripping sweat.

In my mind, I had accepted the fact that my body was beginning to break down. Reaching the highest level in tennis while playing singles was not in my future. Even though playing doubles was my new focus, I signed up for singles tournaments, but with lower expectations.

Montserrat Alonso was a player from Chile who I was rooming with and also who I played against in the tournament. She was the type of player who hit everything back and didn't miss. She wasn't known for hitting winners, but nothing got past her. In tennis, that type of player is called a counterpuncher or counterpusher. She could run across the court from side to side and never tire. She was difficult to beat because she could outlast people and wait for them to wear out and miss.

I had a big forehand and serve, and though my mobility was limited due to the knee surgery, my endurance was good. We played on a hard court, and at over ninety degrees Fahrenheit and with all the humidity, the match was less a game of skill and more a test of survival. In the lower-level pro tournament, each player was given just two bottles of ice water and one Gatorade. We had to pay for extra. I bought—and drank—a lot of bottles of water over the course of those three weeks.

I played a three-set singles match against Montserrat and won. I then needed to face off against my doubles partner and good friend Francesca Segarelli from the Dominican Republic. She and I had played against each other in singles in juniors and also played with each other as partners in doubles. We had won a junior tournament together in Jamaica, and she was someone I grew up with since we traveled all around the Caribbean together. When I played against her in the quarterfinals of this tournament she ended up beating me. I couldn't stop her powerful backhand, which was her strongest shot.

With more games and tournaments ahead, I needed dry clothes to get through those weeks. The hotel laundry service was expensive. After every match, I hung my clothes out on the balcony to dry.

Then, Francesca and I teamed up for a doubles match—and we ended up winning the tournament. That was the first time I partnered with her in a pro tournament. That was huge, not so much because of the tennis but because of the conditions. The sweltering heat made it feel like the Hunger Games, where the last girl standing up there, holding the trophy, was the only survivor.

When I played for multiple weeks in Europe or the US, there was usually travel time involved. I recovered during that time. Playing those tournaments in Mexico offered little recovery time. The tournament started on Monday; the finals were on Sunday, and the next tournament started the next day. Sometimes the tournament director gave us a break and started the tournament on Tuesday. Still, the schedule was exhausting. After three weeks of play in the Mexican summer heat, I was wiped out and ready to go home.

Three-week stints took a toll, and I seldom played well the entire time. I might play well the first week, but the next two weeks were hard. I was tired. Playing well consistently week after week is very difficult.

TENNIS SEASON

The tennis offseason is short compared to other sports. The WTA (Women's Tennis Association) offseason is only four weeks long, from late November until the Australian Open, which is usually the second week of January, with players traveling out to Australia typically the day after Christmas to play in the handful of warm-up tournaments before the Grand Slam. Thanksgiving through Christmas is typically a tennis player's downtime, though they can find tournaments every week of the year somewhere in the world. With so little time to recuperate and work on their game, players are stretched to the max. Those at the highest level get slightly more time to recover, possibly preventing injuries from overuse.

Though players and coaches know they need more time off, the rules will probably never change. As long as organizations can make money from the games, they'll continue running them as often as they can get players to show up. The public isn't aware of how often players participate because tennis isn't publicized like other sports. The four annual Grand Slams get ample media coverage, but fans must seek out all the other games. It's not like football, basketball, and hockey, where fans tune in for a season and then get a break—or move to the next sport. For players and the most avid fans, tennis is truly year-round.

TURKEY

Like Mexico, Turkey also ran weekly tournaments for a while. Theirs were worth $10–$15,000. Playing in so many tournaments gave players a chance to increase their ranking without traveling from one city or country to the next.

I had never played in Turkey and didn't know what to expect. Just once, I'd played in Morocco, and I expected a similar experience. Safety was a concern, so my mother—who hadn't traveled with me in a while—went along for the three-week trip.

Like in Mexico, the hotel was safe and very nice. It was a true all-inclusive resort, and all the meals took place in the same restaurant. However, the resort town of Antalya, on the Mediterranean Sea, was freezing. That was odd and unexpected. Antalya is known as a vacation destination, lined with luxury hotels and beaches. Tennis players who were used to dressing for Florida temperatures donned long-sleeved shirts, jackets, and gloves. They wore tights under their skirts to keep their legs warm.

Turkey is home to a lot of stray cats. I'd walk out of the hotel, and a dozen cats would be just outside the door, staring up at me. It was creepy. In the hotel lobby, we were offered tea. Apparently, tea was the country's beverage of choice because it was everywhere. The Mediterranean food was healthy and delicious—sweet, spicy, and savory medleys with lots of vegetables.

Playing in North America, I was used to seeing many of the same girls. In Turkey, most of the players weren't familiar, so I took the occasion as an opportunity to make friends, starting with my doubles partner.

In doubles tennis, players are responsible for finding partners before the tournament. The organization released the names of players a few weeks ahead of time, and I scrambled to find a good partner. Sometimes I couldn't get anyone to commit ahead of time, and I'd find someone at the tournament. There was a deadline for signing up, adding to the stress. Everyone was trying to double up with the best player available, so it was hard to get a straight answer right away. A player might tell you she was not sure and would get back to you the next day. Meanwhile, she'd reached out to other players and was waiting to hear from them. The next day, you'd follow up, and if she still couldn't commit, you'd have to reach out to other players. The worst was when someone agreed to play doubles with you and then changed her mind because she got an offer from a higher-ranked player. This could happen after you had already turned down offers from other players.

Tennis players at the highest levels make agreements ahead of time, committing to play a certain number of tournaments together so they aren't stuck searching for partners at the last minute. At my level, girls sometimes made agreements but then broke them depending on how well each game went. If your partner didn't perform well, you might look around for someone else. Top players are consistent; those striving to reach the top can have good days followed by bad ones. The other issue is the changing schedules. You can't count on a player to be in the same tournaments you're in from week to week.

I found a player on the list, Anita Husarić from Bosnia, who had won some tournaments and had a good ranking. She agreed to partner with me, and so we met up, practiced, and had good chemistry immediately. Encouraged, I went into the first match energized. I had never met Anita before or talked with her much in the past. I'm thankful she spoke and understood English well.

The tournament was played on red clay, which is slower than a hard court. We won the first match. Then we won the second. Then we won the third.

In the finals, we played against the best doubles pair in the tournament, the number-one seed. To everyone's surprise, Anita and I won! This was the first week of the tournament, and I was excited to keep going. Unfortunately, Anita had agreed to play with someone else during the second week. I couldn't believe it! We had played so well, and now I had to find another partner.

We didn't do well the second week or the third. I went from the highest of highs to the lowest of lows. When you're winning, you want to keep playing. When you lose, you want to leave the tournament as quickly as possible. If you're committed to staying for three back-to-back tournaments, you can't leave until you've played your last game. You might lose the first day and then have to hang around for a week, waiting for the next tournament.

Friends who didn't travel for sports would ask me about the countries where I played. They were more interested in the sights a typical tourist would visit.

"Did you go to the Eiffel Tower? The Colosseum?" they'd ask.

When I was winning, I'd take a little time to enjoy the country. Not much because in the back of my mind, I felt guilty for taking time away from tennis. When I was losing, I didn't feel like I deserved to enjoy the sights.

After my final loss in the third week, I couldn't wait to leave Turkey.

In tennis, a "journeywoman" is a player who hasn't reached the top level of the sport but travels week after week, playing in tournaments. Since they aren't winning a lot of money and don't have sponsors, they have to conserve their resources. They often share expenses by rooming with other players, for example. Many journeywomen (and journeymen) are older than the typical pro player. Some should have retired a long time ago, but since they've devoted their lives to tennis, it's all they know. The best ones become coaches.

I didn't play long enough to be considered a journeywoman. In my mid-twenties, I saw players on tour who were in their thirties and had been playing since they were fourteen years old and but never went to college or developed other careers. They scraped by, making $1,000 here, $500 there, barely covering their expenses. For those people, tennis is a grind. The money is unpredictable, and you never know when it will all end.

Seeing people living like this motivated me to think about my situation. I had already peaked in my mind, so becoming a star player wasn't in my future. I didn't want the life of a journeywoman, traveling from one tournament to the next, asking my parents for help when I came up short financially, and never being truly independent even as a grown adult in my twenties or thirties.

I was playing in high-profile tournaments now and then, but most of the time I played in minor tournaments. Those games got little media coverage. The average tennis fan had never heard of them. Most importantly, they didn't pay enough to support a pro player, even if they played well.

Looking ahead to the future, all I saw was more stress. More injuries. More financial strain on my parents. Tennis was an extremely expensive career. It wasn't sustainable.

I could focus on playing doubles only and possibly break through to the big leagues, but there was no guarantee.

Tennis was wearing on me. It wears on everyone. The only person considered a winner is the one holding the trophy at the end. You can win game after game and match after match, but unless you're the last player standing at the end of the week, you're considered a loser. Depending on the size of the tournament, only one in thirty-two, sixty-four, or 120 wins.

The more you lose, the harder it becomes to win, especially if you lose in the first round in consecutive tournaments. The mental game is just as difficult, if not more so, than the physical challenges. A player can spiral and go down a dark path emotionally.

When I played, no one talked about the mental and emotional strain tennis players endure. A player dealing with those problems was considered "spiraling" or "out of control" instead of clinically depressed and in need of professional help. Once considered a taboo subject, mental health is finally being talked about thanks to vocal players like Naomi Osaka and Simone Biles.

I wasn't spiraling. I was starting to think ahead about my future and if tennis was really going to be a part of my lifelong term.

SAN LUIS POTOSI, MEXICO

In 2014, I flew to Mexico to play both singles and doubles matches in a tournament. My mother was with me, and she got to see me win the first-round match. The next day, I went out to the court to practice for the next match. I bent down to tie my shoes—and couldn't get up. I was stuck in position, unable to move. Tying my shoes was something I'd done thousands of times. There was nothing strenuous about it. Terrified and in pain, I lay on the ground. People gathered around me; then they picked me up and moved me off the court.

My mom asked for a physio, a physical check-up by a trainer. I lay there for two hours while players and their parents who knew my mother and me came by to make sure we were okay. There was nothing they could do, though. We were in a foreign country, waiting for professional medical help. After a while, everyone went back to what they were doing. I was a distraction, and they had matches to play. I felt isolated and alone, lying on the ground like that. It was as if I, Danielle the human being, didn't matter. All anyone cared about was tennis.

Finally, a medic came to check me out. The slightest movement caused shooting pains through my body, but he couldn't figure out the cause. He and my mom stood me up, and I felt dizzy, as if all the blood was rushing from my brain. I thought I would pass out.

They put me in a wheelchair and whisked me away to a hospital. My Spanish was pretty good, so I understood what the medical staff were saying. After completing a series of tests, the doctor came into the hospital room holding an x-ray.

"You have a bulging disc," he said, "like you herniated your back."

Herniated my back? What was he talking about? I had won the first match and needed to get back on the court the next day for the second one.

"Okay," I said. "Can you give me a shot? What can you do to fix it so I can play?"

The doctor appeared to think my injury was serious, but I wasn't in the mood to listen. One of the nurses gave me a shot and some pills to numb the pain, and I left the hospital. Walking was painful, but I was determined to play. My mother and I had flown all the way to Mexico, and I wasn't going to pull out of the tournament.

Back at the hotel, I went straight into physical therapy mode, stretching, foam rolling, and using my travel stim machine. Back at the facility where the tournament was held, they had a pool. I spent a couple of hours stretching in the water; then I headed to the courts to practice. This became my routine for the rest of the tournament.

I played a close second match, a singles match, but lost. My opponent was Lauren Embree. She was a NCAA national champion with Florida, and she had success on the WTA tour as well. She rarely missed the ball, and her grit and ability to fight for every shot made her a tough opponent to compete against. I couldn't help but wonder if I would have beaten her if it weren't for my messed-up back, since I played really well against her, but I was basically being held together with some duct tape. I stayed in Mexico, played another doubles match, and won. I lost the next doubles match, and we went home.

MORE BAD NEWS

Back in the United States, my mother took me to a well-known medical specialist named Dr. Michael Hatrak, who worked with a lot of pro athletes with sports injuries. He worked closely with players on the Atlanta Braves, Falcons, and Hawks, and the Philadelphia Phillies. He tried some new-age remedies to ease the pain, and they helped. He also gave it to me straight: "You have two herniated discs in your back. You need to chill and give tennis a break for a while. You need to really take care of this if you want to keep playing. If you keep pushing through this without proper care, you could need surgery."

Another surgery. My professional career that I'd worked so hard for, devoted my life to, wasn't panning out the way I'd planned. My body was beginning to break down.

IT WAS ALWAYS GOING TO BE TENNIS

Quitting didn't enter my mind…yet. Athletes had pains, injuries, and surgeries. My herniated discs were another phase in my tennis career. My parents believed it, as all sports parents do. So did the coaches and the other tennis players. I was conditioned to focus on the next match and what I had to do to get there.

No one was going to tell me to quit. Unless a doctor told me that continuing to play tennis would paralyze or kill me, I'd keep showing up for tournaments.

Ninety-five percent of me focused on the next match. Five percent of me considered a life without tennis. My knees were bad. Back surgery might help my herniated discs, but I'd never be as healthy as I had been. I would never play better than I did before my injuries.

A couple of months later, I played a doubles tournament in Indian Creek, Florida.

Victoria Muntean and I were up against Ingrid Neel and Fanny Stollár in the first round. They were significantly younger than us and viewed as the new "it" girls. Ingrid and Fanny were prodigies and the future of tennis at IMG. We lost the match six–4, six–3.

Before we lost the match, I had already lost it in my head. My focus was gone.

I'm not an emotional person. I was trained to hide my feelings, especially on the tennis court. I'd been through plenty of tough matches and kept going, hiding the disappointment that ate me up with every loss.

After that loss, I fell apart. I didn't just whimper; I bawled. I sobbed. My parents were there.

"I'm done," I said. "I'm not doing this anymore. It's over."

My parents looked incredulous.

"What do you mean you're done?" my dad asked.

"You have a tournament next week," said my mom.

They didn't know it, but I had already checked out weeks ago. I was done.

I always planned to leave tennis on a high note. Losing that match scared me. What would my ending look like? Losing to the future prodigies? Losing to players I believed I should be beating or was better than? I didn't want to go out at the bottom, at my worst. I couldn't let that happen. It was as if something snapped in my mind, telling me my tennis career was over—full stop.

I went home to my apartment, logged on to my laptop, and searched for my next career. That was a Thursday. The following Monday, I was in real estate school.

PART III

LIFE AFTER PROFESSIONAL TENNIS

11

THE END OF A DREAM

Professional athletes on team sports have contracts. They live in fear of being cut from the team. They are constantly fighting to prove their value and save their career. Someone else—a team owner, manager, coach—controls their destiny and tells them when they're done. In tennis, there are no teams, no bosses. Every player is an independent contractor playing for themselves. No one tells them when it's time to quit.

A football player past his prime won't continue to get hired and paid. Tennis players can continue playing as long as there's a tournament willing to let them in, a tournament that they can get into with their current ranking or with a wild card from the tournament director or Federation. With so many tournaments in need of players, and with so few eyes on the majority of matches (compared to football, basketball, baseball, hockey, and even soccer), plus the fact that payment is limited to winners, the people running the tournaments can take risks. They will let tennis players in who probably should have retired long ago.

Players past their primes often continue spending money on travel, coaches, and tournaments. No one tells them to stop. I had to take responsibility for myself and my future. I had to tell myself to stop playing tennis.

I retired from tennis in 2015.

REAL ESTATE SCHOOL

After leaving tennis, a new pressure was building in my head: *What am I going to do next?* My parents would want to know, and I needed an answer...quickly.

Mom and Dad would have questions. They'd want to know how I was going to do that—what the steps were to get there. It was how they ran my life and how they expected me to run it. I prepared for those questions, knowing my dad would try to poke holes in my plan. I wasn't jumping into a new career blind. I had done my homework. To get licensed to practice real estate in Florida, I had to pass a week-long course. Then, I had to pass the state exam.

"Okay, well, let's see if you pass," was all my dad said.

I heard many people didn't pass the exam on the first try, and I couldn't afford to be one of them. I passed the course and spent two weeks preparing for the exam. Every minute was spent studying. I gained weight. To release the pressure, I made video diaries on my laptop, documenting my thoughts, my emotions, and the process so when I looked back on it years later, I could remember this crazy period of time of my life.

Passing the state exam was a chance to prove to myself, my parents, and anyone who cared that I was more than a tennis player. I could set my mind to something else and succeed. After hours upon hours of studying chapters and modules, learning all about real estate law and guidelines, I felt ready for the state exam. When I passed the exam, I felt an enormous weight off my shoulders. I had a future after tennis.

The next step was getting a brokerage to represent me.

I was terrified of going on an interview. With no work experience, how could I convince an employer I was worth hiring?

My father was encouraging. "Figure out how what you did in tennis translates to real-world scenarios, Danielle," he said.

I considered what tennis had taught me. What skills did I have? What kind of person had I become?

When I see a CEO on the news blaming someone or something for their company's failures, I'm reminded that good tennis players would never do that. They'd ask themselves, "What did I do that caused this to happen? What could I have done to prevent it?"

Smart tennis players develop a sense of personal responsibility and ownership of situations. I developed these traits. They allowed me to know when to quit, and they'd serve me well in my next career.

I learned to approach interviews differently depending on the person doing the interview. Specifically, depending on how they responded to hearing I was a retired professional tennis player.

Some recruiters found that fascinating.

Good, I thought. *That's a differentiator. They'll remember me.*

Some hiring managers couldn't care less. Their eyes glazed over, and they moved on to the next question.

I left most interviews scared to death and depressed, thinking, *That didn't go well at all.* After one phone interview, I broke down and cried.

I knew how to deal with media interviews after winning or losing a tennis match. Explaining to a stranger why I was the best person for the job was another matter. I didn't know how to prepare and didn't know what I didn't know.

My mind went back to my non-athlete friends from college. While I was playing in tournaments, they were networking, making connections with people who could help them with their future careers. They were working as interns in industries that could hire them after graduation. Some of my friends had part-time jobs in those industries during college or during the summers.

Coldwell Banker in Delray Beach hired me. They gave me a desk, a phone, and a cubicle. I knew how to be mature and professional, but this environment was not at all like a tennis court.

Being a real estate agent was nothing like I expected. For one thing, at real estate school, they didn't tell me about prospecting. No one gave me clients—I had to get out there and find them.

After three days of in-house training, I still didn't understand the job. I sat alone in my cube, wondering what to do. The other agents were twice my age and dressed in suits. They didn't hang around. When you're good at real estate, you don't spend time in the office. You're out there meeting with clients. Doing walk-throughs or overseeing inspections. You are rarely in the office.

Real estate agencies put new people at the front desk to speak with walk-ins, giving them a chance to build a client list while learning the job. I didn't have that opportunity for some reason, and I didn't know where to start.

If an agent was nearby, I listened to their phone calls and tried to figure out how they did their job.

My phone finally rang. A client wanted a listing, a comparison, or something. I didn't understand the question or how to respond.

"Can I have your name, please, sir? I'll find that out for you and then call you right back."

He didn't want to hear that.

"What's the matter?" he snapped. "You should know how to do this."

I didn't know what to say. No one had spoken to me like that before. But he was right. I should have known what I was doing. My whole life was about being prepared. For the first time, I was totally unprepared, and all my weaknesses were exposed. I hung up the phone feeling like a fraud. Sure, I'd passed my real estate school and my state exam, but I didn't know how to be a realtor.

I wanted to cry, to sob, to scream. My eyes welled up with tears, and I fought to keep my emotions in check. I couldn't let the other agents hear me or see me like this.

I never asked my father to save me. My life was my responsibility, and I knew better than to expect anyone to come to my rescue. For the first time, I was out of ideas. And I actually wanted his help. I called my dad.

"I can't do this," I said. "Some guy I don't even know just yelled at me. I don't know what he wants or how to fix it." I kept my voice low so no one would hear, but my father sensed the trembling, the desperation, and the urgency. He went into fix-it mode.

"Danielle, get out of there. Come work for me at my insurance office. You'll learn all the skills you need for your next job. We can fix this."

In the next minute, he laid out his plan for my future. A sense of calm washed over me like a tidal wave. For years, my dad had been telling me what to do. I had accepted his guidance, but the control bothered me. I never felt truly independent. In this moment, when I had struck out on my own and was falling apart, his usual manner of planning my life was exactly what I needed. I loved him so much. My tears of desperation turned to tears of relief.

I was sad too. Working at my dad's office meant going back to Rochester, New York. I had no friends there. I'd be dependent on my parents again. I pushed those thoughts aside and called my favorite aunt Sharon, the real estate agent, to share the news.

She was separated from my dad's brother, Terry, by then, but she and I had remained close. She listened to my plan—my dad's new plan for my future.

"You worked so hard to get licensed, Danielle. Are you going to throw it all away to work for your dad?" she asked.

I didn't know what she was getting at. My father's offer wasn't in real estate. His business was different, but it was office work that could prepare me for something else down the road. Besides, what other choice did I have?

"Come and work with me. Move to Jacksonville, Danielle. Work in my office. I'll show you the ropes. You're going to be great. I'll make sure of it."

I was dumbstruck. First, my father bailed me out. Now my aunt was making me an even better offer. I worried about how my father would respond.

"Don't worry about that," she said. "I'll speak with him. We're going to make this work!"

I hung up the phone a new person. My dad had left me with a sense of relief. Now I had hope. I wasn't stupid and incompetent. I had passed the real estate test and the state exam and was capable of doing the job. The one thing that was missing was a coach. Just like in tennis, I needed someone to guide me in my new career.

Knowing that she and my father agreed this was a good plan for me was a blessing. Technically, she was no longer part of the family. Technically, I could have turned down my dad's offer and moved to Jacksonville without his consent. Going forward in that way was possible, but it wouldn't have felt right. In that moment, I was filled with gratitude for my family, especially my dad. He wanted the best for me, even when it didn't fit his vision.

WATSON REAL ESTATE

Watson Real Estate had its own success school. For weeks, I went through intensive new agent training. My aunt supported me the whole way. What I didn't learn in school she taught me. After a month, I had the foundation necessary to start my new career.

I moved to Jacksonville and stayed with my dad's brother, my uncle Terry, at their house. He and Sharon, though separated, lived in the same community. I'd rarely spent time with my extended family growing up because my tennis career was so intense and all-consuming, so being around Aunt Sharon and Uncle Terry was a treat. Like my mother and father, they were on board with the move and supportive of my goals. I am so appreciative of both of them for this.

Jacksonville was a breath of fresh air. My aunt and uncle treated me like an adult. I could come and go as I pleased and didn't have to constantly check in with them.

Once I finished success school at the real estate agency, I was up and running. Cultivating leads and generating business were the priorities. I made phone calls, met with prospective clients, and held open houses. I knew that if I stuck with it, the job would get easier. I'd develop a client list and get repeat business and referrals. That wouldn't happen right away, so I'd have to grind away for a while—months, maybe years. All while working on Aunt Sharon's team and assisting her with her million-dollar listings. I was able to learn the business and the clientele.

I was used to working hard and putting in the effort for long-term results. Tennis had demanded that kind of work ethic. However, I was passionate about tennis. I looked forward to practicing and drills. When I was healthy and winning, I looked forward to tournaments.

I didn't look forward to real estate. The job was one hundred percent commission-based, so no matter how many hours I worked, there was no money until I closed a deal. Week after week, I'd meet with one person after another and have nothing to show for the effort. In tennis, I was always getting small wins. I'd see my forehand improve, win a game, a match, a tournament. As a real estate agent, I got nothing without a sale.

In tennis, I had a certain amount of control over my outcome. In real estate, anything could go wrong. A client could put in a bid on a property, and the owner could reject it. I'd have a house under contract, and then the inspection report would come back, and I'd find the place needed a new roof. Or the foundation was collapsing. Those setbacks were demoralizing. I'd be back at square one, moving through the process and not knowing when my work would pay off. I felt like I was on a roller coaster with little control over my income and my future.

I thought about what I'd learned at success school. Whatever I earned, if I earned anything, I had to give thirty percent to the brokerage firm. I'd keep seventy percent. I had to shoot for as much commission as possible to make the job make sense financially.

Unfortunately, I never knew how much that commission would be. Clients tried to talk me down. I'd ask for three percent, and they'd offer me two percent. Every conversation was a negotiation. I was making enough to move out of Uncle Terry's and into my own apartment, but I was barely surviving.

I didn't blame people for wanting to save money, but I had to get paid. I felt desperate and vulnerable, sometimes angry. Clients don't respond well to those vibes, so again, just like in tennis, I kept my emotions in check—and held it all in.

When faced with adversity, I struggle to speak up. I was brought up to deal with my problems on my own and not complain or drag other people into them. Anything I say about a difficult situation feels like an excuse. I know this isn't true—reasons and excuses are not the same.

Holding my tongue never gave me the chance to confront people. If we disagreed, I kept my opinion to myself. That behavior didn't serve my negotiation skills, and it made speaking to my aunt about my frustration with the job impossible. She put so much on the line for me, and I didn't want to disappoint her. Even if I could get over that, broaching the subject with her was beyond my skill set.

A NEW OPPORTUNITY ARISES

Real estate agents interact with many people throughout the day. I met folks from all walks of life. They were mostly well off. Many of them were in business.

I was showing a house to a man who worked for a network marketing company. He seemed impressed with my work, which was nice. I was still fumbling around, trying to figure out how to make a living.

"You know, I have a meeting coming up. You should come. You'd be a great fit for this business."

I didn't know what network marketing was, but since no one had told me I'd be great at anything in such a long time, I gave it a shot.

A few people spoke at the meeting. They were enthusiastic and made this new business opportunity sound exciting. *What the heck? I thought. Maybe this is something I can get passionate about.* I certainly wasn't enjoying my current career.

I jumped into the opportunity with both feet. After some training, I was expected to host a PBR, short for private business reception, where I'd invite people in and recruit them to either join my opportunity or become customers of my product. The guy who invited me into this business said I should invite fifteen people and expect half of them to show up. The problem was I hadn't been in Jacksonville long, so I didn't know fifteen people.

However, since moving to this new town, I'd joined Tinder, the dating app, and gone on a few dates. All but one of the men fawned over my tennis career, but we didn't connect on any other level. With no substance to the relationships, I didn't go on second dates. The men continued texting me. So I invited them all to my first PBR. In addition, I invited other people I came into contact with throughout my journey of getting my apartment there. If I had their contact, they got an invite.

Of the fifteen I invited, thirteen showed up at my apartment. My few former Tinder dates mingled with men and women I'd met in passing. I shared my presentation, and people seemed excited about the opportunity. The room gelled as they spoke to each other about the business. Their reactions seemed weird to me, but that was how I had reacted the first time too. It also seemed *too good* to be true. Most of them wanted to join the network and be a part of my team or become clients. That was my first step toward building my business with the network marketing health company.

One man who showed up at the PBR stood out. A month or two before the event, he had taken me to dinner at Bahama Breeze, a tropical, upscale version of Red Lobster.

Javier Walden, who went by Jah, was originally from Oakland. He exuded confidence. During our first encounter at the restaurant, he told me about his work, his successes, and his awards. How he took big-box retail establishments that were struggling and performing poorly and, through his coaching and leadership, turned them around into being the number-one or number-two stores in the country. He really was proud of this and said it with pride. I liked hearing someone be passionate about their results. I could relate. I didn't interrupt him. This was my superpower: active listening to others, being interested, and letting them tell me all about themselves. On dates, I didn't talk much about myself at all. Being a skilled listener was better, in my opinion, than being a brilliant talker. I could learn a lot about a person and be selective and intentional about whether I wanted to reveal much about myself. Most men like talking about themselves anyway. Most *people* enjoy talking about themselves. This was always something that was tough for me. I would get shy sometimes, and people would tell me how humble I was to have the life and upbringing I had, going to IMG, playing pro tennis, and not being more forward about it or braggadocious.

My first impression of him was positive, even when he ordered a drink before the meal. I still had my athlete's mindset that stayed away from alcohol for the most part. When he ordered a second drink at dinner, alarm bells went off. My first thoughts were, *Wow, maybe he needs alcohol to help him relax during this date.*

I left the date confused. Jah seemed so smart and nice. There was nothing about the date that would make it so we didn't see each other after it. I felt minor chemistry with him, but it was still too early. It was still an adjustment for me to go on dates. I could probably count on my hand the number of dates I had been on that were formal like this.

I didn't ask for a second date, and neither did he. Weeks passed, maybe months. When I invited him to my PBR, I was surprised when he showed up. For some reason, during my presentation and the Q&A that followed, he piqued my interest. *Maybe I should give him another shot,* I thought. After all, he showed up.

I reached out to Jah after the meeting via text. He was at Hooters and asked me to join him. This time, we clicked. I was relieved to learn he was just a normal guy who enjoyed a cocktail now and then.

Initially, Jah wasn't interested in being part of my business. He was a district manager for a large corporation and didn't want to jeopardize his successful career. The funny thing was, that was exactly what I was doing! Still working with my aunt as a real estate agent, I hadn't told her about the new business opportunity I was growing. I made excuses to get away for events and managed both jobs simultaneously.

The success I started to have with it convinced Jah to begin working the business with me. After all, I was quickly building a large network in Jacksonville and starting to make money. You know, the kind of weekly checks with commas in them. This was a change from the real estate work, which could take months to get a larger lump sum. This was more regular and frequent. The work was fun and easy. Together, we'd be a power couple, building a business and earning a great living.

Working together, between Jah's business savvy and my enthusiasm and presentation skills, we built a team of fifty associates. As a top team, we were invited to the company's annual awards ceremony in Orlando. I earned a brand-new white Mercedes GLK because of the volume we were doing. We were on top of the world, and the success was finally so apparent, I felt comfortable sharing the news publicly.

I invited my parents to the awards show. By then, I had broken the news to my aunt and told her I would be focusing more on my new career than real estate. This was a really tough conversation for me. She made me feel so good about my decision and was so supportive.

I still think about that time, and I am so grateful for how she handled that news, since everything was going to change. My parents knew I had a different job, but they weren't one hundred percent clear on what I was doing. All I told them was that I was doing well enough to receive an award for my performance and that I was being recognized in front of thousands of people.

Everything was going my way. I was in an amazing relationship with a great guy. We were making money and winning awards.

The only thing missing was my old life back in Miami. I missed the city, the culture, and the people. Jah was also captivated by what Miami could bring us. He loved Florida, coming from working in the Deep South and for almost a decade moving from state to state with every promotion and opportunity. He was in Jacksonville because the Fortune fifty company that recruited him was headquartered there. He was used to moving to get what he wanted. He always loved how well we were doing and believed in the company and the leaders, like I did. We each had our own apartment, but after we started working the business together and becoming serious, we were always staying in my apartment. Our relationship progressed pretty rapidly. I didn't have much experience with serious relationships prior to Jah. You learned about my prior relationships and how all of them ended because I didn't want to be controlled or told what to do. My early time with Jah was a lot of growth and learning how to be in a serious relationship. What is acceptable, what isn't; what is appropriate, what isn't. I was building the plane as it was in the air, and in the beginning there were many times I didn't do the right thing. This was tough for me but harder for him. More so because I'm sure he didn't realize how much coaching would be necessary to make our relationship solid. Jah is five years my senior, and his upbringing and environment was extremely different from mine. There was a lot of growth and understanding to do when getting to know each other better. We knew we wanted to go to Miami and start our life together. We packed up and moved south.

12

FINDING PURPOSE OFF THE COURT

I was naive. There's no other explanation for what we did.

The network marketing recruiter fed me a vision that seemed too good to be true. I followed the rules, did my presentations, and built my network. We were making good money. Miami had everything we needed—it would be an awesome new market for this company, and we were so excited to share the company's message and vision and grow it.

I learned that bringing people onto our team and getting them to buy the products was easy. Getting them to build their own networks was hard. Once they'd purchased the products, they'd struggle to build a team, and they'd give up. So the sales were fewer, and our team was dissolving. The only way to maintain our income was to continue bringing in new people. The whole thing felt like a scheme, but we were told it was legal because people were buying products.

The pay schedule was odd too. Like most sales jobs—and like tennis, too—we were only as good as our last month. With this company, if we didn't perform as well as or better than the previous month, our monthly bonus decreased.

Jah and I saw our incomes decrease, and our business began to crumble.

After a heart-to-heart discussion about the business and where it was headed, Jah and I decided to break free. To achieve the vision we'd been sold, we would have to work many more hours and spend more money on products, with no guarantee of a payoff. We were completely soured on network marketing and needed a fresh start. We needed something more stable, with more of a guarantee, that wasn't one hundred percent commission based. Looking back, we regret diving so deeply into it and pulling so many contacts and family into it. That youthful optimism was rampant in our bodies, and we truly believed we were doing the right thing. We didn't have the presence of mind of what could happen if it didn't work out.

The problem was that neither of us had anything to fall back on. We'd quit our jobs. Worse because we had been doing so well initially, we were living in an expensive high-rise condo in Miami. With no income and lots of expenses, we resorted to paying for everything with credit cards, and we went through our savings.

We got gritty. We ate bologna and ramen. We watched the show *Roots* to cheer ourselves up, thinking, *Yeah, our lives suck right now, but at least we're not Kunta Kinte.*

Curled up on the couch together, watching the characters persevere, put us in a new frame of mind. No one was going to save us. We had to save ourselves. We both refused to ask for help or let our families know how bad things were and what was happening. I could not tell my parents how broke we were and how much we struggled. In desperation to make money, we did whatever it took. No shame, all heart.

Jah started getting up at the crack of dawn every day and driving to construction sites to work as a day laborer. I felt sorry for him, but also proud. He had left a high-six-figure salary to chase a dream with me. Now he was getting his hands dirty, doing manual labor for an hourly rate. Hey, I was there too. If he had to be at the job site at six, I would get up at five to cook him breakfast and offer some encouraging words.

People want to talk about how amazing their relationships are. They seldom talk about the hard times, when things aren't so great. That's when you see who your partner really is and how strong your relationship is. It's easy to get along when everything is sunshine and rainbows. How are you when you are dealing with major adversity? My whole training prepared me for this period of time. I knew I had to maintain a positive mindset and push us daily toward our goal of getting back on our feet. I prayed to God every night and every day to give us a chance and not let us have to tell our families what happened.

I interviewed at Nordstrom, PetSmart, and everywhere else that was hiring. We both drove for Uber when we had any free time. Whatever it took, we did it. No shame. Finally, I got a "normal" job as a front desk clerk for a car rental company. The money was terrible—about $500 a week. Jah was proud of me, though. He told me to hold my head up and hang in there. He was interviewing everywhere, certain that something would come through. This was my first real job. My first W-two job. It was 2015. I believe my starting salary was $22,000. Finally, all this work, belief, struggle, sacrifice, and determination paid off.

It did. He was hired at a shoe store. Not just any shoe retailer—he got a job as the GM of one of the largest DSW stores in Miami, a flagship location. In his mind, as a former regional manager and district manager at bigger corporations, the position was a major step down. The money was good, though, and between the two of us, we were paying down our debt, and were able to pay all of our bills. We ate less ramen and bologna. I thank God for allowing us to never be late on our rent or our car payments during that tough period. From the outside looking in, we were thriving. We still smiled, laughed, and worked out. We kept our expensive gym memberships at the Equinox that we had gotten when we were making a lot of money with the networking marketing company. We didn't want to strip away all the luxuries we had, but we did have to stop eating out completely, and I cooked every meal—not well, but I did. I could follow directions, and that was what reading a recipe was.

I was always on the lookout for the next thing. The rental car company was okay, but standing still in one location eight hours a day didn't sit well with me. I was getting bored, and I felt like I had way more skill than what they were utilizing me for. Generating new business wasn't part of my current job, but I had to find a way to stand out. I talked to my current boss and pitched him on the idea of me growing business for the branch by partnering with other businesses and their concierges. I visited nearby hotels and pitched the idea of offering luxury rental vehicles to their guests at a discount. I was a good talker and was determined to be more than a desk clerk.

Jah suggested I get on LinkedIn. He was already on there, and he had seventeen,000 followers. "Update your resume, Danielle, and get it up there," he said. I didn't know if that would solve my career dilemma, but it was worth a shot. I polished my resume, and he helped me create my LinkedIn profile. Then I posted it and connected with as many people as I could.

I started posting content, not really knowing what I was doing. Before long, a SaaS (software as a service) tech startup reached out. The company's focus was automotive, and I knew enough from working at a rental car company to convince the hiring manager I could take on an account manager role covering the state of Florida. The pay was a massive jump from what I was currently making.

A jump like this was truly magical, and I got the job because of my LinkedIn profile, my current experience, and my ability to sell up my skills into an opportunity that required you to have previous account management experience. I didn't actually have account management experience, but I pitched myself anyway.

I have always pitched myself. On paper I'm never who they want, or the right fit, but when I can talk to someone and sell my skill set and my potential, that is where I really shine. At the same time that I was in offer discussions with this tech company, another company in the natural juice/smoothie industry reached out. They had a manager opening at their Brickell, Miami, location. That role would be in my backyard, and I could walk there from our current condo. *Wow,*

I thought. *Two companies want me at the same time.* I became eager to see which one I could get more money out of. Jah was super helpful in guiding my decision. Even though the manager role may have paid ten thousand more than the auto tech one, the role would be stationary, and I would have to go to a physical location every day. The other role was remote and would be covering a book of business across the state of Florida. It came with a company car allowance, and I would be traveling a lot. He swayed me in that direction because he knew that role would be better for my professional development.

I always tell people if it weren't for Jah, I may not be where I am today. He didn't know me for my IMG days and my pro tennis career, but he helped me so much in the corporate world and in navigating the gymnastics that is corporate America. I was always an entrepreneur, and that was my sweet spot. He helped me take my skills and parlay them into opportunities that would suit me well.

At the end of 2015, I finally told my parents what had been going on in our careers. Jah and I had hidden our financial difficulties from our friends and families for a year. They didn't know we had left the network marketing business behind. Ashamed to admit our failure, we didn't feel comfortable telling anyone about that mistake until we were solidly back on our feet. I was able to give my parents an update that I was proud of. I told them about my time at the rental car place and that I got recruited, and now I managed a territory overseeing eighty car dealerships across the state of Florida. My parents were thrilled and surprised. Since they had been so out of the loop, I'm sure they wanted to ask a bunch of questions, but they didn't. They were just happy to know we were both in great standings since we were living together and splitting our bills. They, too, had grown their agency from scratch and gone through some tough times in the beginning as a new couple. I'm sure they could relate to wanting to get it right and not wanting to admit defeat to their families.

I had a friendly conversation with my uncle Terry about the new job. He'd been in the automotive industry for decades and gave me some good pointers. After speaking with him, I felt as if I was finally on the right path. How cool was it that I was joining the auto industry, my uncle's former field? If you had asked me, I wouldn't have seen this career for myself, but with my uncle's guidance, it turned out to be the perfect introduction to the corporate automotive industry.

THE START OF A NEW CAREER

As the account manager for over eighty dealerships, I spent my weeks driving all over the state. In my first year, I made the President's Club. My sales counterpart, "Sandy," sold into these dealerships, and I followed up with the launch and training on the new products. Once my dealers were onboarded and trained, I maintained and serviced the relationship with the best white-glove service.

"Sandy" was a tyrant. Nothing I did was good enough for her. I was a top performer, with one hundred percent customer retention and zero percent churn, numbers that were unheard of in the industry, but still she would find things to nitpick me for. She had an extremely high standard, and in her previous role she sold and did account management, so she wasn't used to someone else managing accounts she sold. She, too, gave impeccable customer service, and she was known in the state of Florida as the woman with the sourdough bread. She used that as a warm takeaway to give prospective dealers she was trying to close. It worked, and she sold everybody. Working as her counterpart was tough, but it did teach me a lot about business. I just hated that she didn't trust that I would do a good job. I was a top performer always, and I didn't need her putting more pressure on me. I already did that to myself.

Then, in the last month of the year, a group of twenty dealerships canceled suddenly, with no explanation. Overnight, a quarter of my business disappeared. I never learned why they left, but in business, anything can happen. Car dealers are fickle. The competition is tricky. Those dealerships could have moved on for many reasons. They were Sandy's customers, too, and she blamed the lost business on me. Sandy *really* went off, yelling at me, venting and complaining to my boss, her boss, anyone who would listen to her. Since she was a top salesperson, and she held weight, but so did I. I was no scrub, and I was also viewed in high regard. I didn't appreciate her doing this, and I always remembered how it made me feel. I was used to being held to high standards, but I wasn't used to being spoken to that way. From then on, Sandy treated me even worse than before.

I had been keeping my LinkedIn profile up to date and posting regularly. With a regular presence and a brand, I had begun developing a pretty large following. I surpassed Jah's seventeen,ooo, and I had twenty,ooo followers looking at my posts and watching me. People were noticing my posts, and they were commenting on my content regularly. My inbox began dancing. A recruiter reached out to me with a fantastic offer—much more than I was making working with Sandy. I jumped at the opportunity. When you are good at what you do, you *never* have to be concerned if someone else will want you. Results always talk. When you are good, you will always be okay. I learned that through my experiences on LinkedIn and the countless hiring managers and recruiters who reached out to get me on their companies' team. I was flattered, but I learned I should expect this because I am good. I am the best in the world at what I do.

My employer did not take the news well. They accused me of taking everything I learned to work for the competition, which wasn't true. They threatened legal action but had no case.

Once again, LinkedIn had delivered a good job. I was on to another SAAS tech startup. This one was in the series B stage when I joined, and I finally had actual equity in the company. *Now we are talking.* This meant if the company IPOed (went public) or was acquired by another company, I would get paid for my efforts and time there through my stock options.

Around this time, my posts were going viral. I focused on mindset, leadership, overcoming adversity, and all the other lessons tennis had taught me. People I didn't know commented on them and messaged me privately, telling me how my posts resonated with them.

I told my father what I was doing with the platform. He said,

"You're really good at this, Danielle. Maybe you should write a book about it."

This was 2020, during the pandemic. I didn't know the first thing about being an author, but my father had written a book, and the process seemed arduous. Ironically, I had just run into a friend, a mental performance coach for the NBA who I've grown to view more like a big sister. Laura Mitchell Wilde had self-published her book, *The Cosmic Athlete,* right before I reconnected with her in Miami. It was divine timing because we were at the Loews Hotel on South Beach when I told her my vision and goal of writing my book, but I didn't know how to start.

"Go on Amazon and look up KDP publishing," she told me. I got online, and she stepped me through the process while I took notes. It was such a blessing to have her right by me in this moment, when I needed support and guidance, and there she was. We caught up because we met when she used to live in Brickell back in 2016, but she had moved to Los Angeles to begin her work with the Clippers. She was back in town visiting.

Writing a book was my new goal. I dove in and wrote furiously. Within weeks—five, to be exact—I had a book. It wasn't perfectly polished, but it had all my insights for separating yourself from the masses on LinkedIn and building a standout brand that would cause recruiters and hiring managers to pause and want to inbox you with an opportunity. I launched the book as a lead magnet for my LinkedIn career coaching and branding business I started called Headstrong, and it took off quickly. Organizations began to reach out to me to speak to their sales and customer success teams. Sports organizations began reaching out, and for me, that was a full-circle moment. The first one was the Florida Panthers, and then it was the USTA (United States Tennis Association), and then others.

Writing that book taught me another lesson: you can give people a road map of exactly how to solve their problems and reach their goals, and most of them won't follow it. Most people won't do the work. The people who take that road map and follow it can go any-where they want. They are the ones who do the work.

I learned something about myself, too: I am a person who does the work. A *doer,* not a talker. No matter the outcome, win or lose, I never shied away from doing the work. As long as I maintained that ethic, I could never be a failure.

I took on clients for my business and learned quickly that some of them would never do the work. That was fine with me because I could do it for them for a hefty fee. Other clients would take my advice and run with it. It really depended on the person or organiza-tion and how much they wanted to be handheld or just pay to have my team do it for them.

The *Headstrong Podcast,* which I launched in 2019, gave me a plat-form to interview achievers who had overcome adversity. My guests came from different industries and backgrounds. I invited athletes, entertainers, businesspeople, and entrepreneurs to share their sto-ries and motivate my listeners to maintain a positive mindset so they could tackle their own obstacles. The podcast brought in more clients. I was invited to be a guest on other people's podcasts, and their listeners started following me. I could see how my LinkedIn posts, book, podcast, and coaching business fed off each other to drive business. In the meantime, I was meeting interesting people and continuously learning. All while maintaining a serious career in the tech startup space. I was always juggling five or six major things at once but still managed to do all of them with success and recognition.

CINCO DE MAYO 2020

My career was taking off, and so was my business. I had great friends. A couple of my college friends you remember, Bianca and Amanda, threw a virtual Cinco de Mayo party during COVID-nineteen since we were all in lockdown. We drank tequila and yapped and had the best time possible under the circumstances. It felt so good to see them and laugh and reminisce on college days.

Naturally, we talked about our relationships. My relationship with Jah had been solid, but it was the one part of my life that wasn't progressing as quickly as I'd expected. Jah and I had been together for five years at this point. We'd been through more ups and downs than any other couple I knew. Yet we weren't engaged. Marriage was the logical next step. Why hadn't he asked? My friends wanted to know. *I* wanted to know. I hated having to answer this question because it wasn't within my control. If I was doing all the right things to be a wife and he knew that he wanted me to be his wife but just hadn't pulled the trigger, what could I say when this question was asked of me? I always would say, "When the time is right, he will." I stopped putting so much pressure on him to do it faster. That caused arguments.

When I had questioned Jah about what was holding him back in the past, all I got were vague answers. The uncertainty was killing me; since I was getting older, my biological clock ticked ever so loudly, it seemed. I had to know what was next. The unpredictability bothered me the most. It was not as if I wasn't doing all the couples things. I worked, cooked, and cleaned. We'd lived together for five years.

After the virtual party, slightly tipsy, I broached the subject again. My close friends were married or engaged. I wasn't getting any younger. I didn't raise my voice, but it was no secret that I was irritated.

"Fine, fine," he said. We were living in a two-story loft condo. Jah went upstairs and came down with a ring. Turned out, he'd been holding onto it for a year!

Before COVID-nineteen, we had planned to visit Europe. He was going to propose there, he explained. Since canceling the trip, he had been waiting for the perfect time.

He got down on one knee.

"Will you marry me?" he asked.

I said yes. Then I blacked out. Maybe I'd had too many tequila drinks. Maybe I was in shock. Whatever the reason, I don't remember anything else that happened that night.

The next morning, I woke up with a ring on my finger. I glanced at it and screamed, then cried, then hugged Jah. And felt a sense of happiness swarm my body. Cinco de Mayo will always be special for me. I haven't had tequila since.

ANOTHER NEW START

Not long after the engagement, Jah was offered an executive position at a promising tech startup in the cloud kitchen space. The opportunity was exciting, but it meant relocating from Miami to San Diego. I couldn't imagine moving across the country. Florida was my home. Besides New York, I had never lived in any other states. I loved Miami; *I am a Miami girl*. But I loved my fiancé and I wanted to support him. He took a leap of faith to follow me from Jacksonville to Miami back in 2015 when we started dating. If I was going to be his wife and his greatest supporter, I, too, needed to do what was best for him and his career. It helped that the executive package was a massive jump from his current role as a GM of the shoe retailer.

Jah had worked for Fortune fifty companies his entire life and was excited about working for a smaller startup where he could really make a difference every day. He had never worked in startups before. I was on my third at this point. I was so excited for him to experience what I knew startup life to be. Fast-paced, wearing many hats, feeling connected to the mission and the people. Being ready to work long hours but have equity and a feeling of ownership in your work.

I didn't want to leave Miami, but we were engaged. My newest job was remote, so moving wouldn't affect my career. I didn't want to hold him back. He'd left a job for the marketing opportunity. He'd moved to Miami for me. Maybe it was time I paid him back. After leaving a great career to pursue the network marketing gig, this was his chance to rise back up the ladder. Besides, I'd heard good things about San Diego.

They brought him in at a high level and for a lot of money. They paid for the relocation.

San Diego was beautiful, but it wasn't Florida. I never felt safe there. We were in another high-rise condo, but I couldn't walk outside without seeing homeless people. Sometimes I saw people doing drugs on the sidewalk. The weather wasn't what I expected either. Even during the summer, the temperature rarely broke sixty degrees. At night, the temperature dropped, and I froze.

Jah's job was going well. He was among the top performers in the company. I figured I'd get used to California eventually, or we'd move to a different neighborhood. We'd been there about a year and had a routine that included working out together. One day, after about a year of living in San Diego, we were at the gym when his phone pinged. It was a Slack message inviting Jah onto a call.

That wasn't normal. Meetings were prearranged. We got into the elevator and headed back up to the condo.

"Why do they want to do a call right now?" I asked. "Isn't this weird?"

"It's probably nothing," said Jah. He didn't seem concerned. I was worried.

From my office, I heard Jah on the Zoom call.

His boss was there, along with HR. She told him he was being laid off.

I gasped for air, unable to breathe. The call ended, and I heard Jah break down. I'd never seen him like that. He didn't see it coming and was in shock.

I had just been promoted and was making good money. Between the two of us, we could afford a lifestyle we'd never enjoyed in the past. Suddenly, that was ripped away from us. Living in California was expensive, so we needed more income.

Jah didn't waste any time. He got a part-time gig doing deliveries for Amazon Flex. Since I worked from home, I tried to get my work done early and arrange my schedule so I could go on deliveries with him. As stressed out as we were, being together on those drives was a chance to bond. We had conversations and got to know one another even better.

Through my *Headstrong Podcast*, I'd interviewed people in similar situations. Layoffs were common in the technology industry. Seeing my husband go through the experience gave me a new perspective. It was even worse than my podcast guests said it was. I never wanted my fiancé to go through that again.

DAD'S CANCER

In June 2020, my dad called me. His voice sounded shaky.

"Danielle, I have cancer."

The words kept coming, but I didn't hear them. I heard fear, as if he were afraid to tell me about his prostate cancer diagnosis. Like he was afraid of what my reaction might be.

Then, a calm came over me. I felt as if I had come out of my body, leaving my emotions behind. I asked him pragmatic questions: when did he find out? How bad was it? What were the doctors saying?

His demeanor changed, and his confidence came back. This was the conversation he was used to—talking through problems and figuring out how to fix them.

"You're going to be fine, Dad," I said. "We'll get through this."

It was the first time my father had needed my help. I knew how to respond. He'd been reassuring me my whole life. Now, in his hour of need, it was my turn to provide that same calm reassurance.

DAD'S CANCER TREATMENT

I had just gotten engaged. There was no way Dad was going to miss the wedding. I believed that with every fiber of my being. But because of COVID-nineteen and the shortage of medical resources, he couldn't start treatment for a couple of months.

I was still living in San Diego during his treatments, but we kept in touch on the phone. He kept the details to himself and shared little with me or my mother.

Part of the treatment involved taking hormones like estrogen. A side effect was a noticeable change in his personality. Dad became the sweetest, most emotional person I knew. He'd tear up during movies.

My mom joked, "Danielle, have you noticed how nice your father is? Maybe they'll keep him on estrogen a while longer." She was teasing, but I understood the sentiment. Dad was always nice, but the shots made him *super* nice. He was fun to be around. The medication also caused him to gain weight.

Later, I learned my dad had a biopsy and radiation treatments. It would be three long years before his cancer went into remission. He came off the medication, lost all the extra weight, and went back to being the dad I knew and loved, with or without those extra shots of "niceness."

A WEDDING

After so much anticipation, being engaged was a massive relief. I could move forward with the wedding plans. Given a goal, I went into mission mode, planning and organizing every detail. I had a wedding planner, and she did a terrific job managing the event. But every decision, every item on the to-do list, got my attention. We were still living in San Diego, but with my parents and friends in Florida, it only made sense to fly back there for the wedding.

A year later, Jah and I were married in Miami. The wedding was perfect. My father, still undergoing cancer treatment, walked me down the aisle.

We returned to California, but there was nothing for us there. Shortly after the wedding, we packed up and hightailed it back to Miami *for good.*

The Miami Open is a big deal, one step below the Grand Slams. My parents took me to it every year when I was a kid, but I never got to play in it.

In 2023, Break the Love, an organization for tennis enthusiasts, partnered with the Miami Open for Women's History Month. They reached out to me on LinkedIn to host the event. I had never emceed an event.

I was intrigued by the offer but also terrified. Public speaking scared me to death. I could play tennis in front of thousands of people. Put me in front of an audience and ask me to speak, and I fell apart. Turning down opportunities at that point in life seemed silly. The time had come to get over my fear and not let it get the best of me.

I remembered my dad saying that as long as I gave everything one hundred percent, the outcome didn't matter. Focusing on that belief, I accepted the offer and prepared for the event.

The duties included moderating a panel that included Olympic gold medalist Monica Puig and another top tennis player, Jennifer Brady. I had played against Monica in Puerto Rico early in her career and toward the end of mine.

The organizers gave me a script to follow—five pages to memorize. No notes, no teleprompter. I was in the back, getting ready to go out, and incredibly nervous. Monica and Jennifer were nervous too. Like me, they could play tennis in front of a crowd. They could do a post-game interview and talk about tennis. Public speaking wasn't the same. It wasn't something any of us were used to. It was scary.

The three of us took our places on stage, and I started talking. The moment I got that first sentence out, my nervousness faded away. My preparation and practice paid off, and I got through the speech without a hitch. Monica and Jennifer relaxed and did well too. My parents were in the crowd, along with Jah and several friends.

The event got rave reviews. My parents were proud of me, and I was proud of myself. The realization hit me like a ton of bricks: *I could do this.* I could speak in front of crowds and host things and get paid to do it. That day led to more engagements. I hosted an event for the Florida Panthers. The USTA reached out to me to host a tennis event.

MOVING UP AND SLOWING DOWN

Around this time, my employer tapped me to be the face of the company. The position is usually reserved for an executive, like the CEO, but the senior leaders were introverts who didn't want to be in the spotlight. I, on the other hand, raised my hand at every opportunity to address the public.

They gave me a shot, and I crushed it. Suddenly, I was the spokesperson for the automotive division.

While Jah was searching for his next career move, he started a fulfillment business from home. That lasted until he was offered a job at another startup. The company in San Diego was in the series C stage of funding, with a lot of investors, cash, and resources. This new company was pre-Series A. He knew it would be challenging. When a company's that new, employees are expected to work a lot of hours. He worked seven days a week. For a while, we didn't spend a lot of time together, but finally, we had financial stability. I was ready to move ahead with the next stage in our relationship.

From a young age, I had convinced myself that I would adopt a child. The thought of being pregnant scared me. A pregnant woman's body changed so much, and you had no control over it. Breastfeeding freaked me out. Early in our relationship, Jah and I talked about having kids, but it didn't seem like a priority for him. I definitely wasn't ready then, but our years together put my mind at ease. Maybe I could carry a child. Other women did it. With our careers taking off, the time seemed right, and we talked about starting a family. Three months later, I was pregnant.

The at-home pregnancy test said I was pregnant, but I wanted a second opinion. I found a gynecologist and got an appointment for the next day, and she confirmed it.

"Yes, you are pregnant," she said with a smile. "But you have a hematoma."

She explained that I had an internal wound and had to rest.

"No more workouts. You have to slow down. If you continue to stay active, you could lose the baby."

I was crushed. Between the gym and Pilates classes, I was in the best shape of my life. But I didn't question the doctor's advice. I stopped everything and took it easy. Two weeks later, the hematoma had healed, and I was given a clean bill of health.

Being pregnant was strange. I'd always been a vivid dreamer. During my pregnancy, I couldn't recall any dreams at all.

HOSTING THE CONFERENCE IN VEGAS WHILE PREGNANT

In October 2023, I was three months pregnant. Depending on my outfit, people guessed I was three months pregnant, or they didn't notice my belly at all. My height might have hidden my extra weight. Regardless, I was hired to host the Digital Dealer Conference in Las Vegas. Dealerships and vendors in the auto industry come together at the event to talk about the latest trends in digital advertising, retail, and automotive technologies. The offer took me by surprise because I worked for one of the vendors. I let my company know that I was doing it so they wouldn't be surprised to see me on stage at the event.

The opportunity paid off in many ways. For one, it solidified my value with my company. Also, I got a lot of offers from other companies in my inbox. That gave me peace of mind. I was building my own brand outside of the company I worked for. The LinkedIn posts, coaching, podcasts, and now the hosting were paying off. Even if I got laid off, I was confident I'd find work somewhere else.

WHEN WINNING WAS EVERYTHING

For pro tennis players, winning is everything. It's their identity. For many years, it was mine. When I lost, I considered myself a loser.

A failure. Worthless. I believe these feelings of despair are more common in individual sports, where there's no one to blame but yourself when you lose. You can blame your coach, I suppose, but ultimately, you're the one on the court swinging the racket and hitting the ball. Or not.

I cannot overemphasize the single-mindedness of playing tennis, or any sport, for that matter. It consumes you to the point that nothing else matters. In my life now, if I don't achieve a goal, I'm not devastated. I have plenty of activities, events, and people in my life so that coming up short in one area doesn't feel like my world's about to end. When I played tennis, that was how I felt many times.

A handful of women playing at my level when I quit went on to have stellar careers. If I had taken my doubles career more seriously, maybe I could have done the same. It's easy to think that, watching Wimbledon from the couch. I didn't choose that path, and I'll never know. The what ifs can drive you mad. When my mind goes in that direction, I have to let go of the past and remind myself to be grateful for all that I have right now. All that wouldn't be possible if I hadn't left tennis behind.

I have a healthy body, a great husband, and a beautiful little boy. I have a career. I'm an author.

Tennis can turn you hard. The constant competition. The losing. The rejection. The complete focus on yourself. The constant clamoring for that next win, hoping the next game will be the one that changes your life. The sheer desperation to "make it."

I played more games in the US than any other country, but tennis took me to Mexico over forty times, just behind Canada and ahead of Colombia. Then, European countries. From age thirteen through my professional career, I was lucky if I had five weeks off a year. In Miami, I traveled less, but only because I played for the college team.

When I was a student in Miami and Tampa, I had nightmares about keeping up with my studies and playing for Coach Caroline. To this day, I still have those nightmares.

Since then, I've smartened up. I've also learned that I deserve better—the best. I've learned to demand respect from the men I associate with, and I found a man (who's now my husband) who's worlds apart from those guys I dated in school. Thank goodness.

I try not to have regrets, but I can't help thinking if I had stayed away from Miami, the coach, and the painful training sessions, I would have continued to improve. My tennis peaked halfway through my career, before college. It's hard not to think about how my life would have been different if I had stopped comparing myself to other players, had more faith in myself, and bet on myself. I could have gone pro at fourteen. That would have meant giving up my freedom to live with my parents. I'll never know how that kind of trade-off would have panned out, and I try not to think about it. But the possibilities cross my mind from time to time, and it's those times I have to remind myself of all that I've done and all that I have. My marriage. My son. My business. My career. Would all that have been possible if I had chosen a different path? I'm not one to live in the past. I love my life now, and that's where my focus lies today.

I live in the present and focus on the moment. Not the past, and not even the future. I strive to be intentional about how I spend every minute of every day. What I focus on expands to become my life.

EPILOGUE

LIVING MY LEGACY

In late 2025, I took my husband, Jah, and my twenty-month-old toddler, Otto, back to Bradenton. First, we drove past the house I grew up in. The place was run-down—not how I remembered it. I pointed to a front window. "That's where I snuck out of the house at night," I told my husband. He just smiled. He'd heard my stories and was familiar with the few times I'd broken the rules as a kid.

Then we drove to the IMG campus. I hadn't been back in a while, and I wondered whether the Academy had suffered over the years like my old house had.

That was definitely not the case. In fact, the place had grown and blossomed. It was like Disney World. All the buildings had been torn down and replaced with state-of-the-art facilities. The campus was much bigger too. As a student, I walked, scootered, and sometimes took a golf cart between dorms, classes, and tennis courts. Since then, a tram had been installed to transport students, staff, and visitors around the campus. There were still plenty of golf carts too.

Otto ran around the courts where I'd spent so many hours training. The memories energized me, and my husband and son picked up on my energy and seemed just as excited by the place as I was.

We stopped by Margie's office. Margie Zesinger was one of my early coaches, and she's now the head of women's tennis at IMG. Knowing how much she'd supported me in the past, I was thrilled to see her value to the Academy recognized and rewarded.

I took photos of the professional tennis players displayed around the campus. Later, I posted them on my Instagram page and tagged each person in the photos. One by one, the people I tagged began reaching out. There was an IMG alumni event coming up, a banquet to honor the late, great Nick Bollettieri on the anniversary of his passing. Tommy Haas, a former #two ATP player, was the host and organizer, and he wanted to know if I was interested in attending. Yes, of course! I was delighted. What an honor to be invited back to the Academy to rub shoulders with these elite athletes.

A DREAM REALIZED

The banquet was held at the St. Regis in Longboat Key, a short drive from IMG. The Colony at Longboat Key was the site of Nick Bollettieri's original tennis school, Bollettieri Tennis Academy. The Colony had been replaced by the St. Regis, a grand hotel that rivaled the Four Seasons.

We felt as if we were standing on hallowed ground, where it all began. Everyone who was anyone in tennis during the 1970s, '80s, '90s, and early 2000s was in that room. Grand Slam winners. Hall of Fame inductees. Pro athletes and coaches. Among the speakers was the Academy's first student, a woman who looked to be in her seventies. The celebrities included Tommy Haas, Max Mirnyi, Mary Carillo, Christian Harrison, Sabine Lisicki, and Mary Pierce. There were some people from my era and later too.

I worked the room, moving from one person to the next, introducing myself and taking selfies. Then, people began approaching me.

"You're Danielle, right?"

To my surprise, they had been following me on social media. People wanted to speak with me.

Not everyone remembered me, though, either because they had graduated long before I started or because my appearance had changed completely. At IMG, I was a skinny young girl with straightened hair and glasses who tooled around campus on a scooter. Now I was a woman, a wife, a mother, and an author, with a career and a business.

Suddenly, something incredible happened. I went from being the "young unknown" to being the center of attention. I wasn't just a girl surrounded by her idols. I was a grown woman with presence. I was…*important*. I mattered.

The two-hour banquet flew by, and when it was over, most of the attendees left. I found myself speaking with Mary Pierce, a woman I had idolized growing up. Before there was Maria Sharapova, there was Mary Pierce. In 2000, she won Roland-Garros, aka the French Open. Mary represented everything I'd wanted to be.

"Do you want to come to dinner with us?" she asked. Mary explained that she and some of the other guests were gathering after the banquet. She was inviting me to join her and this exclusive group of tennis elites. I had never been relevant to these people, and I was taken aback, but also immensely flattered. Apparently, I had made enough of an impression during the banquet to solicit an invite to a more intimate dinner with people I had looked up to my entire life.

I thought back to my humble beginnings. At IMG, I was the awkward girl. I was the girl who tried to fit in but, for all the wrong reasons, stuck out like a sore thumb. After years of training, practice, and tournaments, I only scratched the surface in the world of professional tennis. Now I was being welcomed into the inner circle.

The dinner was amazing. I made dozens of connections. The pros talked to me, and so did their agents and managers. They spoke with me about future opportunities.

Then someone said, "Hey, Danielle, do you want to hit with me tomorrow?" Other pros joined in, and we agreed to meet up the next morning to play tennis. The way everything fell into place was surreal. It was as if my whole life had led up to being not only accepted but invited to play tennis with my idols.

I called my husband, who was back at home with Otto. I had planned to drive back first thing the next morning, but he encouraged me to stay.

"Have a good time, Danielle," he said. "You've earned this!"

EARNING MY PLACE IN THE SUN

Revisiting IMG was a full-circle moment. I realized how my upbringing at home and the Academy's environment made me the person I am today, a woman who can make things happen for herself.

Taking the initiative to reach out to those tennis stars got me in the room. Once I was there, I didn't cling to the walls. I made my presence known. I had practiced my pitch, uncertain whether I would make an impression or fall flat on my face. I had to put myself out there or I would never know.

The training, the practice, the tournaments, and the mindset work had set me up to capitalize on that moment. I'd been waiting my whole life to be in a room with those people. I didn't squander the opportunity.

When I talked to my dad about the event, he said, "You've been practicing for this your whole life."

He was right. I had overcome the fear of rejection and learned to advocate for myself. I was confident and ready to enter any conversation as if I had nothing to lose.

My tennis years were tough. I didn't achieve my earliest dreams, but I achieved much more. What I learned is a message I want to pass on to you. One that I hope you'll remember and take with you as you move forward in life, whatever your dreams. You don't have to be the best. You don't have to be the most talented. You don't have to be the one everybody thinks will be the superstar. Work hard. Be strategic. Focus on your assets. Don't wait to be chosen, and don't dwell on missed opportunities.

With the right mindset, you can handle everything that comes your way and be a great success. Create your own opportunities. Look for those moments, and take the initiative to make them happen. But understand that you won't be able to do that without training. You have to go through the hard stuff that builds your confidence and resilience so you can walk into any room and feel comfortable talking to people you've never met before, people you've looked up to your whole life.

It is not up to other people to decide your worth. The power and the right to determine your value is within you. Obstacles and rejection might feel like they're holding you back, but they are exactly what's necessary for you to become the person you were meant to be. The most difficult times prepare you for that moment when you need to step up and claim your place in the room.

If you're unhappy with where you are today, make a change now. You don't deserve a life of regrets, of looking back and thinking, *I could have. I should have. I would have.* You are better than that. Use my story and this book as a catalyst to change what you don't like about yourself and your life. Do the hard work to make it better.

And remember, we are all students. We never really "arrive." As long as we continue to take risks, overcome obstacles, and learn, we are students evolving to become the people we need to be in the moment. This is how we prepare for those rare opportunities—the experiences that define the best of who we are and move us forward to becoming the people we were always destined to be.

Now it's your turn. Dream your dream. Take your shot. Where you end up might not be the place you expected, but it could be much, much better. And you'll be ready for it.

ACKNOWLEDGMENTS

Thanks to my parents, Barion and Norma Mills, for believing in me from the start and for the unwavering support. I strive every day to love and support my son, Otto, the way you love and support me.

Thank you to all my coaches, especially Nick Bollettieri, for the impact you made on my life and confidence you instilled in me when I needed it the most.

And finally, thank you to my husband, Jah, for being my rock, selflessly putting me first, and being my biggest fan. Building our lives together has been a dream come true.

ABOUT THE AUTHOR

DANIELLE MILLS WALDEN is a retired professional tennis player, an Amazon bestselling author, a LinkedIn expert, and the founder of Headstrong LLC.

A former Division I athlete at the University of Miami, Danielle competed professionally on the WTA Tour. After retiring from professional tennis, she set out to make a difference for others seeking to reach their full potential in business and in life.

Drawing from her experiences training alongside the world's top athletes and elite coaches, Danielle founded Headstrong, a mindset and career coaching company designed to help others achieve a champion's mindset.

Danielle's first book, *How to Master LinkedIn & Separate Yourself from the Masses,* provides actionable strategies for enhancing online presence and growing professional networks. In her second book, *Scratching the Surface,* she shares her experiences as an IMG Academy student, Division I athlete, and professional tennis player—a life that inspired her insights on mindset, goal setting, and personal branding to unlock career opportunities.

A sought-after speaker, coach, and LinkedIn influencer, Danielle has empowered countless professionals to build strong personal brands, amplify their influence, and elevate their careers.

Follow Danielle at Linkedin.com/in/daniellemwalden.

Contact Danielle for coaching and speaking engagements at headstrongmind.com.

REFERENCES

1   Kelley King, "The Ultimate Jock School: The Education Is Intensive—and Expensive—at IMG Academies, Where Sports Come First and Classes Are Fit into Training Regimens Designed to Help Students Reach Their Athletic Goals," *Sports Illustrated*, November 25, 2002, https://vault.si.com/vault/2002/11/25/the-ultimate-jock-school-the-education-is-intensiveand-expensiveat-img-academies-where-sports-come-first-and-classes-are-fit-into-training-regimens-designed-to-help-students-reach-their-athletic-goals.

2   Joel Drucker, "Nick Bollettieri, Force of Nature and Tennis Academy Pioneer, Dies at 91," Tennis.com, December 5, 2022, https://www.tennis.com/news/articles/nick-bollettieri-force-of-nature-and-tennis-academy-pioneer-dies-at-91.

3   Anthony Cormier, "Management Shake-Up Hits Bollettieri Academy," *Sarasota Herald-Tribune*, January 13, 2009, https://www.heraldtribune.com/story/news/2009/01/13/management-shake-up-hits-bollettieri-academy/28686523007/.

4   Prior to NIL (name, image, likeness), college students couldn't profit from the commercial use of their identities. They chose to be college students or professional players. Students who played in professional tournaments also couldn't keep all their winnings, but only enough to cover their tournament expenses. See https://www.ncaa.org/sports/2021/7/9/name-image-likeness.aspx.